G000094864

The Parents' Pony Book

The Parents' Pony Book

Carolyn Henderson

Illustrations by Ann Pilgrim
Photographs by John Henderson

J. A. Allen

British Library Cataloguing in Publication Data
Henderson, Carolyn
  The Parents' pony book
  1. Livestock: Ponies
  I. Title
  636.16

ISBN 0-85131-495-3

Published in Great Britain by
J. A. Allen & Company Limited,
1 Lower Grosvenor Place, Buckingham Palace Road
London SW1W 0EL

© J. A. Allen & Company Limited, 1990
Reprinted 1995

No part of this book may be reproduced or transmitted in any way or by any means, electronic, or
mechanical, including photocopy, recording, or any information storage and retrieval system,
known or to be invented, without permission in writing from the publishers. All rights reserved.

Typesetting and make-up by
T & S Typesetting, 1 South View, Hewish, Avon BS24 6RW.

Printed in Hong Kong by Dah Hua Printing Press Co.

Contents

List of Illustrations

List of Plates

Acknowledgements

My thanks go to Corrinne, Chimene and Amanda Ferras for being such good models; Mrs Pauline Davies of Pett Farm, Sittingbourne, Kent, for the use of the photographic location; Tom and Judy Featherstone of Birchalls the Riding Shop, Maidstone, Kent, for the loan of equipment; and especially to my husband, John Henderson, for ideas, encouragement and for taking the photographs.

1 Is a Pony a Practical Proposition?

If you have picked this book up in desperation because your child wants a pony and you do not know a wither from a fetlock – do not despair. Every year thousands of children plead with unsuspecting parents to make this dream come true. Some parents ignore the plea in the hope that it will go away, but others relent and let themselves in for the pleasures and perils of pony keeping.

It is for those parents that this book is intended, because with common sense, basic knowledge, and careful planning a pony can become a much-loved member of the family. He can also be at best a costly mistake and at worst the cause of much heartbreak . . . so before you commit yourself, it is vital to take a long. hard look at whether or not a pony really is a viable proposition.

I have assumed right from the start that yours is an average, animal-loving family with an average income, therefore this book is not intended for the few lucky ones with five acres of land behind the house, a Range Rover in the garage and three hunters in the stable block. They do not need it. For ease of writing I have also assumed that – as ponymania hits more girls than boys – it is your daughter who is the would-be owner, but the advice applies equally to your son.

For a start, how old is she? If the answer is not at least ten, then the pony really should be put on the list of 'when you're a bit older' projects. A pony is more than a pet; it is a demanding, time-consuming working animal that takes a lot of looking after. His care demands physically hard work if you are going it alone, although there are other ways of keeping a pony, such as full or part livery – more about these kinds of 'horsey hotel' systems later. It takes a mature and responsible child to accept all the ties that go with a pony, and it is not fair to expect really young ones to cope.

If you have given in to pleas for animals before and then been landed with their care when the novelty wore off, think twice. It is all very well cleaning out the hamster or walking the dog, but feeding, grooming and exercising a pony is quite a different prospect.

By now you are probably wondering if you can interest your daughter in ballet or macrame instead of ponies. It is not meant to sound such a grim prospect, but a pony really is a huge responsibility, and once you have him he relies on you for all his needs. If, however, you are ready to keep your side of the bargain, he will give you a great deal in return.

It is also essential that your daughter has a good grasp of the basic riding and handling skills and knows how to feed, groom and generally look after a pony. She should, therefore, have spent at least a year having weekly lessons at a school approved by both the British Horse Society and the Association of British Riding Schools. Most good schools are happy to let children help under supervision, and, if weekends and holidays mean you never see your daughter owing to the attractions of the riding school, so much the better; she has probably already learnt some of the skills needed to cope with a pony of her own.

If you are reasonably happy in your own mind that your daughter could manage, have a word with the owner of her riding school to make sure, and if you find him or her easy to talk to, cultivate the relationship. A friendly instructor can be a godsend when it comes to finding a pony and making arrangements for how and where it is going to be kept, not to mention giving you the reassurance of knowing that if a problem comes up that you cannot cope with, help is only a 'phone call away.

The next thing you have to consider is whether or not you are going to get on with the pony. It's no good saying 'I'm not going to get involved with it', because you will. For every mum or dad who has stated categorically that the pony will be strictly their daughter's province, I will show you half a dozen more who find themselves doing everything from feeding him before it gets dark in winter to fetching pony nuts from the local feed merchant. That is the bad news. The good news is that most people enjoy it; it opens up a new circle of friends, because you are bound to meet other parents in the same position. With ponies, one thing invariably leads to half a dozen more.

Initial Costings

If you have managed to get this far without being put off, one question will probably stand out above all the rest; how much will it cost? Unfortunately there is no set answer beyond the basic one that a pony will cost a lot more to keep than a dog. If your daughter has been telling you that a pony is really

You're bound to meet parents in the same position

cheap because he only needs grass in the summer and hay in the winter, both she and you will have to accept that, in reality, it is much more expensive. A lot of ponies, particularly hardy native types (that is ponies indigenous to the British Isles, like the New Forest and Welsh) can and do exist perfectly happily on staple diets of grass and hay. But it is not enough; they also need what is known as hard feed, i.e. grain feeds or ready-made compounds such as pony nuts.

Your pony will also need a new set of shoes every four to six weeks, which will cost around £20-£28 a time, and worming every six to eight weeks at £5 a time. Annual flu jabs and tetanus boosters will be about £10. If you are sensible you will insure the pony not only for accidental death, loss and theft but also for third party liability and vets' bills. You cannot put a pony in the back of the

Riders with mounts the correct size. Amanda rides the 12.2 hh Toby, and Corrinne is mounted on Taffy, a 14.3 hh Welsh Cob

car and take him to the vet's surgery, and if he needs X-rays or lengthy treatment you could soon be talking in terms of three figure bills.

Keeping ponies is not cheap, but it need not be astronomically expensive, either. To start with let us look at what it would cost to buy a pony and his basic equipment.

What Size Pony?

The first thing to decide is how big a pony to buy. Obviously this depends on the height, weight and experience of your child, but generally the bigger the pony, the bigger the price. One problem is, of course, that children grow

Too big and strong

amazingly quickly, and you might be tempted to buy a bigger pony than your daughter needs on the theory that she will grow into it. Do not succumb to this temptation; if he is too big and strong it will only lead to problems.

The riding instructor is the best person to advise on what height to go for, but let us assume you have decided she needs a 13.2 hh pony. That means he is 13 hands and 2 inches; a hand is 4 inches, and horses and ponies are always measured from the withers (the bump at the base of the neck) in a perpendicular line to the ground. A 13.2 hh pony, therefore, is 4 ft 6 in high at the base of his neck.

Buying a pony is a lot harder than buying a car. There are no hard and fast rules to say that a pony of such and such a height and such and such an age will be such and such a price. It depends on looks, temperament, age, ability, performance record and to some extent even which part of the country you live in. As most sellers expect to haggle over the price (they may knock about £50 off their asking price) it can be totally confusing first time round: but as a general guide, at current prices, a good, average 13–13.2 hh all-rounder will cost approximately £500-£800 without any of its tack and equipment.

Tack and Equipment

Sometimes you will be able to buy a pony's tack (horse parlance for saddle,

Rider too small for the horse. Taffy is much too big for Amanda

bridle and other bits and pieces of saddlery) with him, and if it is in good condition and has been well looked after that can save you a lot of money. A fair price for a good quality, secondhand saddle, bridle and headcollar, the latter being the pony's equivalent of the dog collar and lead, would currently be about £150-£250.

If you have to buy the whole lot brand new, it is time to count the cost again. Good quality (both English and foreign) tack is expensive, but it is the only sort worth buying. There are plenty of cheap foreign goods on the market, and you will often see them at auctions, but they are frequently of inferior quality and can be dangerous. A new, good quality pony saddle will be about £275. Stirrup irons and leathers and a girth, which goes round the pony's belly, will add up to about £30, and an adjustable nylon headcollar and lead rope about

£8. A new bridle, complete with bit and reins, puts another £50-£60 on the bill. These are average prices for new goods, and it is worth shopping around; most saddlers are happy to advise you and will show you how to get the most for your money.

Another way of cutting the cost is to buy secondhand tack through newspaper and magazine advertisements or auctions, but this can be risky unless you know what you are looking for: worn stitching or stressed leather is not always spotted in the heat of the moment, so if you are budgeting for secondhand tack take an experienced person with you. Again, it is worth asking your local saddler, as they often have used tack of guaranteed quality for sale.

Once you have bought your pony and tack they will need looking after and keeping clean. If your daughter is used to helping round the stables or has done one of the excellent 'own a pony' courses that most riding schools organise, she will probably already have her own grooming kit. If not, that is another

Rider too large for the pony. Toby can take Corrinne's light weight, but is obviously too small for her

£10–£15 to spend on brushes for the pony and cleaning materials for the tack. Although it seems a lot to spend in one go, you can take comfort from the fact that as long as it is properly cared for, good tack lasts for years. In fact it should still be going strong when your daughter has outgrown her first pony and needs something bigger to replace him.

If she is going to look after the pony herself you also need to include the cost of essentials like feed buckets, plastic dustbins in which to store the feed, and haynets – about £12. If the pony is going to be stabled at night in the winter you might also have to provide a wheelbarrow, fork, shovel and yard broom. Some livery yards provide mucking out tools, but many DIY places expect you to supply your own.

Vetting and Insurance

These are two more vital points to be considered when working out the initial costs. When you have found your prospective pony, you must have him checked over by a veterinary surgeon before you hand over the money; the vet will examine him thoroughly and check that he is healthy, or 'sound', for the work you want him to do. Even if the pony lives nearby the vet's fee will probably be about £50–£75. That might sound a lot, but remember that a vet trains for five years before even starting in practice: you are paying for his skill, time and experience, so look upon vetting as an investment.

A lot of people will tell you that it is not worth having a pony vetted and that all you need to do is get a knowledgeable person to look at him. By all means get your expert to look at him first, and hopefully spot any obvious defects and problems, but remember that only a vet can tell you if there is something wrong with a pony's heart or if he has an eye defect.

The pony should also be insured whether he is valuable or not. He will quickly become part of the family, and although the heartbreak of finding there is something wrong with him cannot be measured in financial terms, illness and accidents are costly. Again, some people will tell you it is not worth paying insurance premiums on a £400 pony, but if the worst happens and the pony dies, you will wish you had. Even more important, you will be covered for third party insurance and vets' bills. The latter can be very hefty, and if you have to call the vet out several times and pay for X-rays you could easily end up with a bill for as much as the pony cost you in the first place. That is, of course, looking on the black side, but it is safer than assuming it will never happen to you.

The recent experience of a family I know underlines the importance of

If he has an eye defect

insurance. Their daughter was out riding on her quiet, reliable pony when a car came up behind them in the lane. The driver was considerate and slowed down and, as the pony was obviously not bothered by the car, pulled out to overtake. Just at that moment a pheasant shot out from the hedge under the pony's nose, and he leapt sideways in fright. The rider was, luckily, unhurt, but the pony smashed one of the car's headlights and cut his leg. He was still lame after a few days and the vet had to be called in.

Those few seconds landed the girl's parents with a £65 bill for repairs to the car and another one of £43 from the vet. By the time they had written out cheques totalling £108, the £80 they had paid to insure the pony earlier in the year seemed like a reasonable investment.

It pays to shop around for insurance cover, as for everything else. Usually you are better off dealing with one of the specialist horse and pony insurance firms, many of whom advertise in the horsey magazines – but be sure to read the small print in the policy. For instance, while many companies offer insurance against 'loss of use', the definition of what that involves varies considerably. It is also not worth insuring the pony for more than you paid for him, as most policies will only pay out either the sum insured or market value, whichever is the lesser sum. The premium quoted will depend on the pony's value and what he is used for, but, as an example, one of the better known companies quoted £90 in May 1990 to insure a £450 pony for one year against everything from vets' fees to death and tack loss or damage.

Although it might sound horrific at first, once you examine it, the cost of buying a pony is not so bad. You can probably buy him and his equipment for less than the cost of a family holiday, and I guarantee he will give you more pleasure than two weeks in the sun.

2 Housing the Pony

Once you have decided that a pony in the family *is* a practical proposition, it is all too tempting to rush off and read the 'Horses for Sale' advertisements. Read them by all means, but before you even think of looking for your pony you must sort out the question of where he is going to live. To a large extent the living accommodation you can provide will dictate what sort of pony you can buy, because if he is going to spend most of his time at grass he needs to be fairly hardy. Thin-skinned, elegant show pony types cannot cope with living out all the time and are not usually suitable first ponies.

Welfare organisations like the Horses and Ponies Protection Association (HAPPA) exist to rescue and, where possible, rehabilitate ill-treated animals. Often these horses and ponies are not the victims of deliberate cruelty but of ignorance, but it does not mean their suffering is any the less. One of HAPPA's strongest pleas is for people to ensure they have enough properly fenced grazing with adequate shelter before they buy a pony. Their casebooks are full of stories of ponies tethered on poor quality exposed grassland; tethering is an unacceptable way of keeping a pony, so forget any ideas of your future purchase being a useful lawn mower!

Keeping a pony at home can be the perfect system, but few families can manage it. Apart from the fact that ponies need at least an acre of land per animal, there are issues like planning regulations and how open-minded the neighbours are. To a horsey person, a well-maintained muckheap can be a source of pride, but to someone who lacks your enthusiasm it can, not surprisingly, be a smelly eyesore. For most people, the answer is to rent grazing from a friendly farmer or at a specialised livery yard, which is a kind of horsey hotel where you either do everything yourself, the staff do it all for you or you carry out some tasks and rely on them to do others for you.

Ponies are naturally herd animals and it is not fair to keep one on his own.

Not only will he get lonely, he will show it in all sorts of inconvenient ways – like jumping out or pushing through the hedge to look for a friend. So try to find somewhere where another pony is kept or a horse or pony in your area that needs a companion.

Your pony will need to be visited at least once and preferably twice a day, so, if you are thinking of renting land, work out the cost of your time and travel and add that to the rent – which will probably be about £5 or £6 a week. Even though you may not plan to use it, you must have access to a stable in case of emergency. If the pony falls ill or has to be confined for any reason, he will need more than a field shelter. The average combined rent for stabling and grazing is about £10 a week, but you might be able to do a sub-letting deal. Perhaps the stable owner will let you pay a small retainer on condition that you can use a stable in emergencies while the owner uses it for another animal the rest of the time.

Livery Yards

For first time pony-keepers it is probably best to keep him at livery. He will have the company of other horses and ponies and you will have the comforting back-up of someone who knows more than you do. Reading a book that will prepare you for problems you are likely to face is one thing but being confronted on a dark winter evening with a pony who has cut himself is quite another.

If you keep your pony at livery you will also meet other 'pony families' and be able to key in to a network of moral support and practical help. Babysitting circles have nothing on the pony varieties: if you get a family emergency and have to dash off somewhere it makes life a whole lot easier if you can 'phone another pony parent and ask them to look after your animal for the evening. Horsey people are an obliging lot . . . everyone knows it could be their turn next time!

Types of Livery Yard

There are four kinds of livery: full, part, DIY and working.

FULL LIVERY

Full livery is expensive, because the yard staff do everything for you and you are paying for the privilege of turning up to ride your groomed, fed and mucked-out pony. You will not see much change from £40-plus a week, not to mention additional costs like shoeing. Half the fun of having a pony is becoming involved with his care, so most people do not even want to think about full livery.

DIY

DIY means that you do all the work but pay for the rent of grazing and, perhaps, stabling and the cost of food, bedding, if he is stabled part of the time, and incidental costs like worming and shoeing. As a rough guide, an average cost for a pony who is stabled at night in the winter is £20 a week, less if he is hardy enough to live out all the time – though even then he will need extra food.

PART LIVERY

Part livery enables you to get involved with the pony but have some of the responsibility taken off your shoulders. Tasks are shared between you and the livery yard staff and costs worked out accordingly; some are more flexible than others. You need to make a definite arrangement and stick to it, otherwise everyone gets confused and the poor pony is the one who suffers. Perhaps the staff will check him over and feed him for you, and catch him when the blacksmith comes, leaving you to do a second check and, in winter, perhaps a second feed and pick his feet out. But do not expect to be popular if you want to change your requirements all the time, because efficient stables run on routine.

Costs for part livery vary according to who does what and the facilities offered. A good livery yard I know in the south-east is probably fairly typical in its outlook: the owner charges £10 a week rent for grazing and the rent of a stable in the summer, when the ponies live out all the time and rarely need supplementary feeding, and £30 a week in the winter, when the ponies are out in the day, stabled at night and get hay and two feeds a day. The yard is responsible for feeding, mucking-out, turning-out and bringing in, and the owners take care of exercise, grooming and tack cleaning.

WORKING LIVERY

Working livery is offered by some riding schools, but, quite honestly, is more trouble than it is worth, no matter how good the establishment. It means that they look after the pony for you in exchange for being able to use him for an agreed number of hours a week. In theory that might sound like a sensible idea, but in practice it can lead to horrendous problems. For a start, you will find that the riding school will probably want to use him at weekends, when they are busiest. That, of course, is when your daughter will want to ride him, too.

And even if you can come to an amicable arrangement, you will get to the stage where she resents other, perhaps less competent, riders using her pony.

Choosing a Livery Yard

As with all things, there are good and bad livery yards. Some riding schools take horses and ponies at livery and if the one at which your daughter is learning has a vacancy this could be your best solution. But before you commit yourself, ask some of the other livery owners if they are happy there: be prepared for a few grumbles, because you cannot please all of the people all of the time. Do their ponies seem happy and healthy and can they get advice if they want it? Are liveries allowed to use facilities like schooling areas at appropriate times, or do you end up paying for an indoor school you can rarely use? Does the school charge a reasonable amount for feed and bedding or does it add on a hefty whack? You should not expect to pay any more than in your local feed merchant: the school saves you the time and inconvenience of fetching and storing, but should save money itself by buying in bulk. You cannot demand they pass the saving on to you, but nor should they make an extortionate profit.

If your riding school does not take liveries they may be able to recommend a suitable yard. Another idea is to look in the Horses for Sale column in your local paper (it will soon become addictive reading: you will see everything advertised from horses to saddlery and forthcoming shows). The sort of yard you will be looking for is a friendly, well-run type of place that caters for children and ponies: one that is advertised as a competition or showing yard would be too high-powered, too expensive and probably not terribly interested in taking you and your pony.

If you hear of somewhere that sounds suitable, contact the owners and ask if you can have a look round. Even if they do not have any vacancies it is worth doing a reconnaissance, because you will then have something to compare with other yards. If someone there suddenly sells a pony or moves elsewhere you will be in an ideal position to say yes or no if you are offered the vacant box. Most popular yards keep a waiting list and it is worth adding your name if you really like the place.

First impressions are quite important. There is no such thing as a permanently immaculate yard – though some, especially hunt stables and racing yards, come pretty close. But if you drive up a muddy, rutty track through poached fields (i.e. muddy and cut up), fields fenced with sagging barbed wire and inhabited by miserable-looking ponies, you would be best

The distinct impression that you're the one being interviewed

advised to spend the next thirty seconds thinking up a good excuse for turning round and heading home again.

Some yards are quiet, others always have plenty going on, but if you have arrived at a hectic time you should at least get the impression that it is organised chaos. Have a quick glance round: is anyone smoking? There is never any excuse for that on a stable yard, because it is an unacceptable fire risk. Does everything look reasonably tidy, or are there wheelbarrows left all over the place and forks lying on the ground waiting to be trodden on?

You can tell a lot from the person who owns or runs the yard. If you get the distinct impression that you are the one being interviewed, it is not such a bad thing. Conscientious livery yard owners will want to know exactly what you expect from them and the staff, and what sort of pony you are hoping to buy. The horse world goes round by word of mouth, so you could even find yourself with the telephone numbers of a few owners with ponies for sale.

An obvious question to ask is how much it will all cost, but you should also check on how much grazing is available and how many horses are kept on it. If ten horses and ponies are herded on to two acres it is beat the retreat time again. Ask to see the fields (having first mugged up on the next section about choosing one) and check on arrangements for worming. Most good yards insist that they worm your pony and charge you afterwards, because that way they know that every animal is done regularly.

Most yards also have a farrier who visits regularly. As well as being convenient, this can save you money. Farriers usually charge travelling expenses and it works out a lot less when divided between four or five than when you have to pay it all yourself. Your pony will need shoeing every four to six weeks and even if his shoes are not worn down he will need his feet trimmed back. Many yards will keep an eye on them for you and add your pony's name to the farrier's list when they need doing, though you should always take the ultimate responsibility yourself.

Do not be too put off if the yard owner seems a bit formidable at first meeting. She (or he) should not be rude, of course, and should be pleased to answer questions because it shows you are worried about your future pony's welfare, but to run a yard and be responsible for a mixed group of animals' welfare means you need eyes in the back of your head. One of the best yards I know is run by a lady who has the reputation of being a real dragon, but she looks after every horse as if it was her own and can tell at a glance if something is not quite right – often before the owners notice! The very best yards put the horses' welfare before the owners' whims, so if you are paying someone for their experience and expertise take notice of what they say.

If you want to double check on a yard you can always ask your daughter's riding instructor to have a look round for you, providing the owner is happy about it. Most good ones are always pleased to show off their yards, because they know that recommendation by word of mouth is often the best kind of all.

If you find your ideal yard and there is a vacancy, take it. The best places do not have much trouble filling empty boxes and you might come back in four or five weeks only to find that you have missed your chance. Some owners might offer a couple of weeks grace before asking a retainer and others will want one straight away; in either case it should not be any more than the basic rent, minus any services or food, and will often be just a token sum. When you are doing your sums, remember to check whether the yard has to add VAT to your bill. Many do not, but the bigger yards sometimes have to and it can make a surprising difference to the monthly bill.

Whether you are going it alone or opting for a livery system, you need to make a careful check on the grazing. In an ideal world we would all be able to keep our ponies on perfectly maintained pasture with solid, wooden post and rail fencing. Sadly, life is not like that and to a certain extent you have to find the best you can and make the most of it. Even so, there are fields to avoid like the plague, and ways and means to turn the adequate into the perfectly satisfactory.

Choosing a Field

When looking at a field, you will be able to get a pretty accurate impression of its suitability even if you are not an agricultural expert. Is it poor and muddy, with bare earth clearly visible? Is it full of long, reedy grass? Both mean that your pony will not get much food value from it and you will have to supplement his diet with more expensive foodstuffs than will be needed with good grazing.

The field needs adequate drainage, as boggy land means the grass will get churned up and your pony could be prone to mud fever or cracked heels; skin disorders that arise in wet weather. If choosing a field in the autumn or winter your own common sense will tell you whether or not it is going to be boggy, but if you are field-spotting in hot weather keep an eye open for clumps of marsh grass, which grows in places that are wet most of the time.

Is there a lot of ragwort in the field? If so, either be prepared to find another field or put in a lot of hard work. Ragwort is poisonous and must be pulled up by the roots and burned. Deadly nightshade and yew are also poisonous.

Just to prove what contrary creatures ponies are, too much good grazing can be as harmful as too little. Ponies will happily gorge themselves on rich grass – it starts to grow in April and is at its richest and best from about the middle of May to early June – and too much of it can cause a painful and crippling disease called laminitis or fever in the feet. Do not turn down a good quality field (they are few and far between!) but be prepared to restrict your pony's grazing by stabling him for part of the time or moving him to barer pasture during the 'danger period'.

Ponies are greedy little beasts who can hear a bucket rattle miles away, but they are also very fussy eaters. Pastureland is made up of a mixture of grass, clover and other plants, and ponies will only eat the ones they like. You can tell which they are quite easily, as some areas will be short and grazed right down while others are long and untouched. It often helps to graze a pony field with cattle, because the cattle will keep the long grass down.

FENCING

You will quickly find out that lots of old sayings must have been coined by people who kept ponies. 'The grass is always greener on the other side of the fence' is one of them: stout, safe fencing is vital, because ponies are no respecters of anything that looks flimsy. Some of them are the most amazing escape artists; I once knew a pony who would lie down and wriggle under any kind of wire. The tiniest gap in a fence will be exploited by a determined pony, who will push and shove at it until he has made a hole big enough to get through.

The best kind of fencing is a thick, natural hedge, which not only forms an impenetrable barrier but also offers shelter against wind and rain in the cold weather and flies in the summer. Sadly, they are not very common, so if you find one you have every reason to feel satisfied with yourself. The alternative has to be some kind of man-made fencing and most pony books will tell you that the only really acceptable kind is stout, wooden post and rails. Certainly it is the best, and again, if you can find it, make the most of it. But few farmers go to the expense of putting it up and paying a lot of money to fence someone else's land is not always a viable proposition.

Most fencing today is some kind of wire, which sends a shudder to the heart of the truly virtuous but does not have to be as bad as all that. As long as it is taut, post and wire fencing can be adequate; avoid sheep wire and barbed wire if you can, the former because a pony can put a foot through it and get stuck and the latter because it is obviously dangerous.

Electric fencing is another alternative and is especially useful for dividing a large field into small sections so that each can be alternately grazed and rested. Ponies are remarkably sensible about most things and have a strong instinct of self-preservation. You need to introduce your pony to an electric fence by leading him up to it and touching his nose against it; he will get an unpleasant but harmless shock and afterwards will stay away from the fence of his own accord.

GATES

While looking at the fencing, check the gates, too. They must be properly hung not only to provide a safe barrier but to save your time and temper. It is no fun for you or your daughter to find yourself struggling with a heavy, sagging gate while a greedy pony tries to push his way out to get at the feed bucket. In theory it is not a good idea for a gate to open on to the road, as it means you have to cope with traffic every time you lead your pony in and out. There is also the point that it makes life a lot easier for potential thieves if they can park a box or trailer, load your pony out of his field and simply drive away. In practice you do not always have a lot of choice, but if there is a choice of gates use the one that leads into the farm or stable yard even if it makes you walk a little further. It goes without saying that gates should be padlocked at all times when the pony is in the field – and make sure they cannot be lifted off their hinges by determined thieves or vandals. Sadly, there are some people who think it is funny to let horses and ponies out of their paddocks.

FIELD SHELTERS

Shelter is important for the grass-kept pony, not only in the bad weather but in the summer when he needs protection from flies. Everyone will tell you that the best protection is a thick, natural hedge, which is perfectly true, but unfortunately there are not a lot of them about and most people have to rely on man-made solutions.

You might be lucky enough to find a field that already has a shelter, but if not ask the owner if you can put one up. All the horse magazines carry advertisements from firms who sell and erect stables and shelters and many will visit your proposed site and give a free quote. Shelters need to be sited on well-drained areas and positioned so that the prevailing wind does not blow straight on to the occupants. They should have three sides; narrow doorways are dangerous, especially if more than one pony is using them. Squabbles can lead to kicks, banged hips or one pony being banished.

Do not be surprised if your pony prefers to stand alongside his shelter rather than actually going inside it during even the hardest winter weather. Ponies naturally prefer to be in the open and will still benefit from the shelter it offers. Nine times out of ten he will go inside in the summer, when the flies can be a real plague.

WATER

Your pony will need a constant supply of clean, fresh water. He will drink around eight gallons a day, but ponies are so fastidious that he would rather go thirsty than drink dirty water. The best arrangement is water piped to a trough with a covered ball-cock; every time he drinks, the trough automatically fills up again. The ball-cock must be checked regularly to make sure it is clean and working properly.

If you do not have a trough you are faced with the prospect of organising another water supply. Some people use old baths, but they are not a very good idea – the sharp edges round the rim are just the right height to cut a pony's legs. If you have to use buckets, stand them in an old tyre to ensure they cannot be knocked over, and remember that they must be kept full of clean, fresh water. Keeping a pony thirsty is one of the cruellest things you can do, so in winter be prepared to break the ice and, if necessary, replace the water supply at least twice a day.

Grassland Management

Actual pasture management is a mixture of common sense and specialised knowledge. If you are renting a field from a farmer, make sure you both know who is responsible for its maintenance: usually he will look after the bigger jobs like harrowing and fertilising and expect you to carry out the daily checks and removal of droppings. Both these are vital jobs.

It is a fact of life that all horses have worms, but a proper worming and pasture care programme keeps them under control. Your vet will advise you on the former and the latter is common sense coupled with a little knowledge-able help. Hopefully most of us have enough of the former to get by and can find out the rest from experts like the Ministry of Agriculture, Fisheries and Food Agricultural Development Advisory Service, which will be listed in the 'phone book.

Removing droppings from the field is one of the most boring jobs, but it must be done regularly. It is all too easy to put it off, but pasture, where droppings are allowed to lie, quickly becomes 'horse-sick', and picking up the piles twice a week, say, is a lot easier than having a mammoth wheelbarrow session! If you really hate it, it is one of the tasks that younger children can be bribed to help with, or if you are expected to do the job as part of a DIY livery, it is a lot more fun to have a weekend work party.

It is important that you check your field properly every day. Walk round the fencing to make sure there are no loose nails on which your pony could hurt himself, or weak gaps in the fencing where he can push his way out in search of pastures new. Remember, too, that sometimes people throw litter into a field without thinking; tin cans and broken bottles can do a lot of damage.

If the field is next to a house or land where people are going to be cutting grass, make sure they do not throw the clippings over the fence. Your pony will think they are lovely, but because they ferment quickly they can make him ill. This is not something a non-horsey person will know about, so keep your eyes open for keen gardeners.

If you are expected to take responsibility for all the pasture care, or are lucky enough to have your own land, get in touch with your local Ministry of Agriculture ADAS expert or ask your feed merchant or a local farmer to put you in touch with someone from one of the well-known agricultural firms. They will send someone out to take soil samples for analysis, and will then be able to tell you what you need to put on the land and when to do it.

Grass needs to be fed and most people fertilise in March and mid-summer. Before you do so, make alternative arrangements for grazing as you will need to keep your pony off the land for about three weeks after it has been fertilised. You could split your grazing into two with the help of portable electric fencing – this is a good idea in any case, as it allows you to graze one section while resting the other for six or seven weeks.

Weeds and poisonous plants are another problem you will have to deal with. Some can be sprayed, but do not do this without taking expert advice and finding out exactly how long you have to wait before the field can be grazed again. The best way of getting rid of unwanted guests like ragwort and dock is to pull them up, take them away and burn them; do not just leave them lying there. Again, many hands make light work and 'ragwort parties' can give you an excuse for a celebration afterwards!

Three other jobs need to be worked into your schedule if you are to get the most out of your grass: topping, harrowing and rolling. Topping simply means cutting areas of long grass, which ponies will not eat. You can probably do this yourself, but the easiest way of dealing with the other tasks is to ask a local farmer to do them for you. Harrowing is done around the end of February, weather permitting, and pulls out dead vegetation so the soil can breathe. Rolling packs the soil around the grass roots and helps it to grow and, as with harrowing, the farmer can tell you the best time to do it.

Stabling

The work involved in looking after a pony who is stabled part of the time is dealt with later on, but when looking for somewhere to keep your pony it will help to keep a few guidelines in mind.

The combined system of pony keeping, that is when he is out in the daytime and in at night in winter and perhaps out all of the time in spring and summer, is one that works well. The stable is really his bedroom, and just as you would not be happy in a room that was too small and either let water or was too draughty, neither will he, so you need to make sure that the stable is adequate in size and the protection it offers.

Stalls, where the pony spends all his time tied up, are not worth considering. Your pony needs a loose box big enough for him to turn round comfortably, lie down and get up again without a struggle. This means the floor area should measure about ten foot square, though a small pony of 12 hh or less will be all right in one about eight foot square. When he is standing in the box he will need at least three foot six clearance above his head and the doorway should be wide enough for there to be no risk of him banging his hips as he goes in and out.

The best stables are brick-built, but strong timber is perfectly acceptable.

Ponies are happiest in their natural state

Do not be tempted by converted garden sheds: they will be cheaper than the real thing but will not be strong enough. The smallest pony can be surprisingly strong and a kick can do an amazing amount of damage to a flimsy building – let alone the pony if his hoof goes through the wall. Most floors are concrete, because it is cheap and tough, though you might find brick or compacted earth in old farm buildings. The floor should have a slight slope to allow for drainage and the drains themselves kept unclogged.

Windows should be positioned higher rather than lower in the stable walls to allow for good ventilation without exposing the pony to draughts. They should not contain glass unless it is wired glass or otherwise protected. Any light fittings or switches should be covered and out of the pony's reach. I once knew a pony that experimented with eating a light-bulb; luckily he spat it out without hurting himself, but it could have been a different story.

Check that there are no protruding nails or bits of wood or metal inside the stable and that the bottom half of the stable door has two bolts, top and bottom. Ponies are clever little souls and soon learn how to undo bolts – some people will tell you that all you have to do is fasten it with a lead rope clip, but there have been cases of ponies fumbling at these and getting them through their lips.

Keeping a pony can and will fit in with family life, but you do need to be realistic about the time and money available. Ponies are happiest living out-doors in their natural state and as long as you have shelter and an emergency stable when you need it you should all survive quite happily.

3 Which Pony?

When you have your prospective pony's accommodation sorted out, the real fun begins – because you can start deciding what sort to look for. Buying a pony is not easy because there are so many variables involved, but ignore the doom and gloom merchants who will tell you horror stories about shady dealers and hidden defects, and be prepared to be patient.

Important Qualities

Everyone wants the perfect pony, but unfortunately he does not exist. Ponies, like people, all have their good and bad points and what you have to do is work out which good ones are vital and which drawbacks you can put up with. For a first pony, the important things are that he is sound, well-behaved and easy to handle. Looks are not so important, though his basic shape (conformation) has an effect on how he is likely to stand up to work.

No pony is a saint, despite what you might think from reading the advertisements, but he must be well-behaved and good-tempered; you do not want one that bucks or pulls, and it is no fun dodging a lightning pair of heels every time you go round behind him. He and your daughter have got to like each other, because, hopefully, they are going to be friends.

He could, of course, turn out to be she. Many people will tell you to buy a gelding (a castrated stallion) because they are generally believed to be more reliable than mares, but in my experience it is very much down to the individual animal. The theory is that mares can be unpredictable when they come into season, and some *are* affected. Geldings are often more affectionate – mares can be a bit aloof – but against that there are a lot of people who swear that a good mare is the best horse or pony you could wish for. Your best bet is to be open-minded; to simplify matters, however, I refer to the pony as 'he' throughout this book.

24

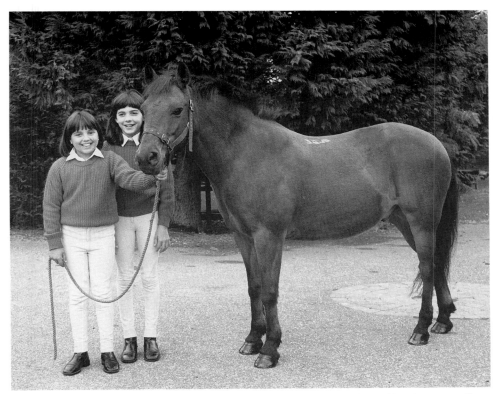

Toby, a 12.2 hh, 12-year-old part-bred Welsh pony has proved himself to be an excellent mount for children. He is shared by Amanda (8) and Chimene (10) Ferras. Toby's freeze mark can be seen on the saddle area

One thing you should never gamble with is the pony's safety in traffic. Some are frightened of lorries or other big vehicles, and whereas an experienced adult might be able to cope, it is a risk no parent should be prepared to take. Unless you live in splendid isolation on top of a mountain, you are going to meet traffic on the roads. Not all drivers are considerate towards riders, often through ignorance, so a traffic-proof pony is a must.

Remember that if your pony lives out you will need to catch him to ride him or check him over. Some ponies are easier to catch than others, and some have good days and bad days. My first pony used to wait until I got about two yards away from her then scoot off and canter three or four circles round me. If I waited patiently while she had her fling, she would then come to a halt and stand meekly while I put her headcollar on.

Without wishing to put you off, there is a chapter later in this book on pony problems which looks at ways of dealing with ponies who do not want to be caught, but if your daughter is going to be managing on her own much of the time, or your purchase will be living in a large field, 'easy to catch' should come near the top of your priorities list. You can solve the problem, or at least alleviate it, but it is better if you do not have to.

Likewise, your pony should be reasonably well-behaved with the farrier – or you might find he will refuse to shoe him. You cannot blame a farrier for refusing to handle a pony that kicks or, even worse, throws himself on the ground. There are some farriers who like a challenge, but given the choice most will opt for the quiet life.

Age

Age is another aspect you need to consider, though you do not need to be too narrow-minded about it. A lot of people will tell you that a first pony should be between seven and ten, and certainly that is a good range. But do not discount a pony older than that, because many work happily into their late teens and even longer. You do, however, have to be practical and think ahead; if you buy a pony who is 13 and your daughter outgrows him in a couple of years it might be harder to find the right home for him. As a guideline, be happy with a pony up to 12 and certainly do not discount an older one if he seems right in every other respect.

It might seem tempting to buy a young pony so that he and your daughter can grow up together, but it is more likely to be a recipe for disaster. A four- or five-year-old will not have the experience or maturity of an older pony and is likely to still find life pretty exciting. Handling and riding youngsters is an art in itself and should not be attempted by novice owners and riders. Occasionally you get an old head on young shoulders who disproves all the theories – the steadiest, most reliable horse I have ever had came to me as a just-broken four-year-old – but this kind is the exception to the rule.

Colours and Markings

Colour is a matter of personal choice and one that I do not take into account. For some people, though, it is important; perhaps they do not like greys or chestnuts. There is an old saying that 'a good horse is never a bad colour', and in my book the most sensible way of interpreting that is that if a pony suits you it does not matter if he is pink with blue spots.

The most common colours are grey, bay, brown, chestnut, dun, palomino, piebald and skewbald. Grey horses are always called grey, never white – it is another horsey peculiarity. Even the one in the famous whisky advertisement is officially grey! It is an attractive colour, but can involve more work and for that reason some people avoid it. A grubby grey pony somehow always looks dirtier than a grubby brown one and is prone to grass and stable stains. Grey horses get lighter with age, so an iron grey (dark grey) four-year-old can be a totally different colour four years later.

Bay is an attractive, solid, popular colour. Basically brown to red-brown with a black mane and tail, it is common to all breeds. Bays officially have black 'points', that is mane, tail, ears, muzzle and legs.

Brown is self-explanatory: the catch is that a black pony will probably be officially brown because of brown hairs on his muzzle or in his coat. Again, it is a solid, attractive colour. Bay and brown coats often have a lovely shine to them in the summer.

Chestnut is an orange-brown colour that varies from light to a dark shade known as liver chestnut. Chestnut horses are sometimes unfairly labelled as being 'hot' or excitable, and some people will run a mile at the sight of a chestnut mare in particular.

Dun is a beige-brown colour, often with a gold tinge to it. Dun ponies often have a dark mane and tail and a dark stripe called an 'eel stripe' along their backs.

Palomino ponies are particularly pretty or unacceptably flashy, depending on your taste. They have gold coats, officially the colour of a newly minted sovereign, and cream manes and tails.

Piebalds and skewbalds are often known as coloured horses. Some love them, some hate them; I've had two and they were both exceptionally nice-tempered, talented animals, so I am a fan. It is often said that for some reason they are good jumpers; certainly mine were, but I cannot think of any reason to prove the theory! Some people disdainfully refer to them as 'gypsy ponies' because of their popularity with travellers. When you think of the pride the true Romanies take in their horses, it is probably a compliment.

Piebalds are black and white and skewbalds brown and white. Sometimes you get ponies that are brown, black and white; if he has more brown that black he is officially skewbald, and if it's vice versa you have got a piebald.

Ponies may also have white markings, notably on their face and legs. An irregularly shaped patch of white on the forehead is called a star; a stripe is a narrow white mark down the face; a blaze is a broader white mark; a snip is a small white mark between the nostrils, and when the majority of the head is white it is called a white face.

You might be told to avoid ponies with socks or stockings. Socks are short white markings on the legs, and stockings longer ones. The only explanation with any logic in it for this is that white legs often end in white hooves and the horn, the substance of the hoof, is stronger if it is dark. But it is not really worth bothering about, despite the old rhyme: 'One white sock, buy a horse, two white socks, try a horse, three white socks, look well about him, four white socks, do well without him'.

Pony Types and Breeds

Your pony will live out all or most of the time. It is the most natural, and therefore the best way of keeping him, but you need to be sure that he is the type who can cope with this system. Forget elegant show pony types, who in any case are usually too 'sharp' for novices, and think in terms of a pure or part-bred native pony. Do not worry if his owners have no knowledge of his breeding; if he is sensible, well-built with a good coat and is already living happily the way you intend him to, you will be all right.

Britain's native ponies have a well-deserved reputation throughout the world for their suitability as children's ponies. The breeds all have their own characteristics and it is often possible to guess a pony's origins by looking at him even if his pedigree is officially unknown. Welsh ponies, for instance, have pretty heads and a certain sparkle about them, known as 'presence' in horsey jargon. Exmoor ponies have pale muzzles, called 'mealy muzzles' because they look as if they have dipped their noses in a bucket of bran, and often pass this on to their descendants.

You can, of course, opt to buy a registered, pure-bred native pony. Either look for one that is advertised as such, or contact the relevant breed society, which often has lists of ponies for sale. If you are put in touch with a breeder, do stress that you are looking for a reliable first pony, not a youngster.

Just as mongrels are as affectionate and loyal as pedigree dogs, so ponies of mysterious breeding can be as suitable for your purpose as pure-breds. Let us take a look at the British breeds and their characteristics, so if a pony is described as, say, part-Connemara you know what type he is likely to be.

CONNEMARA

Originally a native of Ireland, the Connemara is now bred in England and has been successfully exported all over the world. He stands about 13–14.2 hh and is usually grey, though he can also be bay, black, brown or dun. His bonus points are that he usually has a nice free-moving action and a good length of rein: in other words, you do not feel that there is nothing in front of you when you get on his back, as can be the case with short-necked animals.

DALES
The Dales is a chunky chap, the heaviest of Britain's native breeds. Usually around 14 hh and dark brown in colour – though you see grey ones too – Dales ponies have a docile temperament. They also make good harness ponies . . . do not dismiss the idea, because many pony parents end up driving an outgrown pony they do not want to part with!

DARTMOOR
Do not be fooled by the Dartmoor's prettiness; he is a tough cookie who is happiest living out. Standing around 12.2 hh and being fairly narrow, he is the

A Dartmoor pony

ideal size for a small child's first pony. Nimble and quick on his feet, he often excels as a gymkhana pony and all the ones I have known have been good jumpers.

EXMOOR
The Exmoor lives out so happily it seems a shame to stable him. His coat is so dense it is virtually waterproof and, despite his size – about 12.2 hh – he is strong enough to carry a man. The only drawbacks, which breed enthusiasts will hotly dispute, is that some Exmoors have a stubborn streak and because of their short, thick necks they can be a bit strong for a small child.

FELL
Fell ponies look like slightly smaller, lighter versions of their Dales cousins. Usually around 13 hh to 14 hh, they are sensible and sure-footed, two characteristics which mean you will often be given one to ride if you go pony trekking.

HIGHLAND
Highland ponies are between 13 hh and 14.2 hh and will carry any member of

A Highland pony

the family; they are such good weight-carriers that in their native Scotland they are used to carry shot stags weighing around 14 stone. Their talents lie in fields demanding strength and stamina rather than agility.

NEW FOREST
Enthusiasts say that the New Forest pony is the ideal mount for a child. Between 12.2 hh and 14.2 hh, they are usually sure-footed and reliable, and the biggest plus is that they are so used to traffic they are normally very safe on the roads. Ponies are run on the Forest by owners with grazing rights and are rounded up at regular intervals for branding or sale at the New Forest Beaulieu sale.

A New Forest pony

SHETLAND
The Shetland is the smallest native breed and has a measurement system all to

himself – he is measured in inches, not hands. The average height is around 38–42 inches at the withers, but he is incredibly strong and hardy. Obviously his small size means the Shetland is only suitable for small children, but he can be *too* strong for many children, and he must be treated like the proper pony he is, not like an overgrown dog.

A Shetland pony

WELSH

Welsh ponies are often described as the most beautiful of our native breeds, and certainly they are extremely popular both here and abroad.

They are divided into four categories, Welsh A, B, C and D. The Welsh Section A, or Welsh Mountain Pony, is the smallest at about 12.2 hh and, like the ponies in the other sections, has a beautiful finely-chiselled head that shows nineteenth century infusions of Arab blood.

The Section B, or Welsh pony, can stand up to a hand higher and was originally developed for shepherding on the Welsh hills.

A Welsh Section A pony

The Welsh Section C and Section D are more substantial than the first two sections, the Section D or Welsh Cob being the larger of the two. Usually active, hardy and a good jumper, he stands between 14.2 hh and 15.2 hh and makes a great family horse. The Section C, or Welsh pony of Cob type, has a height limit of 13.2 hh and is often an ideal second pony.

Looking for the Right Pony

Buying the right pony demands some detective work, and there are four main avenues to explore – recommendation through word of mouth, through a riding school, through advertisements in the local paper and horse magazines and from a reputable dealer. There are also horse and pony auctions held regularly throughout the country, but though they can provide an educational (and sometimes upsetting) day out, you should not consider buying your first pony this way.

A Welsh Section B pony

Many horses sold at auction are genuine, but you do not get time to try them properly and it is really a bit of a gamble. Buyers who know what they are looking for can get a bargain, but the inexperienced are more likely to end up with problems.

Word of mouth is one of the best ways to find a pony. Contact your local Pony Club; your riding school should be able to put you in touch, or contact the Pony Club headquarters at The British Equestrian Centre, Stoneleigh, Kenilworth, Warwickshire CV8 2LR. The secretary of the local branch may know of a genuinely outgrown pony whose owners want a good home for him, and word soon spreads along the grapevine.

Your riding instructor is also likely to know of suitable ponies that are on the market. You might even be offered the chance of buying one of the school ponies, though this has both advantages and disadvantages.

The advantages are that your daughter will already have ridden and handled

A Welsh Section C pony

him and so they should be comfortable together. The disadvantages are that riding school ponies can change quite dramatically when taken out of the school discipline and environment; many settle happily, but you have to be prepared for a Jekyll and Hyde situation at first. A pony who is used to being ridden in large groups, often taking the same place in the ride, can object to being asked to work on his own, and as his workload is likely to decrease in private ownership he may also become quite a lot livelier.

Your third option is to look at ponies that are advertised for sale. It is an exciting and nerve-racking process, but as long as you keep your wits about you and get advice from an experienced person there is no reason why you should not be successful.

When scanning the pages of the local paper or *Horse and Hound* (the weekly magazine that is the bible of the horse world) you will probably see advertisements for horse agencies. Some of these are excellent and work in a high-tech way by providing buyers with printed lists of potential buys free of charge. It does not cost anything, but it is a bit like buying insurance through a broker or a house through an estate agent in that it introduces a third party.

Last but not least, think of visiting a professional dealer's yard. There are dishonest horse dealers just as there are dishonest people in every business, but remember that dealers have a living to earn, and if word gets round that they only have horses with behavioural or unsoundness problems they will not get many customers. Good dealers have good trial facilities and will want to make sure that the pony will suit you; you may also get the chance to see several ponies on one journey.

Looking at prospective purchases can take up a lot of time and petrol, and unless you do some thorough groundwork it can also take a toll on your patience. Make your initial inquiries as thorough as possible, because that way you will be less likely to waste your own and/or the seller's time.

Before you pick up the 'phone, make a checklist of things to ask.

1. What is the pony's height, age, sex and colour? Double check, even if these are stated in an advertisement. You would be amazed at how vague some people can be, and it is no fun spending an afternoon going to see a supposedly 13.2 hh pony that barely scrapes 12.2 hh.

2. Would he be a suitable first pony? Do not worry if you find yourself being interviewed about where you plan to keep him and if you have anyone to help you: it is a good sign that the seller wants to make sure the pony would be well looked after.

    Be scrupulously honest about your daughter's riding experience. If you get remarks like 'he can be a bit strong' or 'he's really a second pony but he'd be OK if she's a good rider' it is best to thank the seller and politely say it sounds as if the pony would be more than your daughter could cope with.

3. Is he reliable in traffic and is he easy to box, catch and shoe? Listen very carefully to the answers. The pony described all in the same breath as 'good in traffic but he doesn't always like lorries' is not the one for you.

4. Does he have a nice temperament? The only answer you should settle for here is a firm 'Yes'.

5. Does he have any vices? Vices are behavioural problems like weaving, crib-biting and wind-sucking, all of which will make the pony unpopular on any yard, difficult to sell on and may also have an effect on his condition.

    A pony who weaves sways from side to side in his stable, usually over the door. A crib-biter hangs on to doors, fence posts and anything else he can get hold of with his teeth; this vice may also be accompanied by wind-sucking, when he gulps down air.

6. How long has the seller owned the pony and why is he for sale now? Hopefully he has been with them for at least a year and has been outgrown, but there are other perfectly good reasons for a pony being on the market. Parents who give in to demands for a pony without making sure it is not a passing enthusiasm might find a child loses interest when the realities of all the hard work hit home. And, of course, people's personal circumstances change.

   Do not be worried that you are prying. A genuine seller will be pleased to answer your questions because it shows that you are a genuine buyer.

7. Is the pony sound and open to vetting? Do not be satisfied with any answer but 'Yes'.

8. If your first impressions of the pony are favourable, would the seller be prepared to let you bring someone more experienced to look at him? Again, this should not be a problem, though do not be surprised if you get a warning that several people are interested in the pony – it is all part of the gamesmanship!

9. Check the price and ask if it includes any tack or rugs. If the answer is 'No' that is fair enough, but if you are told they might be available you have a possible bargaining point.

10. It is rude and unnecessary to ask someone what is wrong with a pony, but there is a magic formula which never fails. Simply explain that you know no pony is perfect and do not expect to find one – could the seller tell you any funny little habits or peculiarities you should know about?

    The reaction to this varies. Some people swear blind the pony is absolutely perfect and never puts a hoof wrong, while others will say, perhaps, that he can be harder to catch in the summer when there is plenty of good grass about. Occasionally you will be told that the pony previously described as bomb-proof will not go near a tractor or a lorry, in which case it is time to grit your teeth, suggest that he might not be a suitable first pony after all and thank your lucky stars that you did not waste time going to see him!

Taking a Pony on Loan

It is possible that you may come across a family who for various reasons cannot keep a pony – perhaps all their children have outgrown him – but want to put him out on loan rather than sell him. This is a system that has both pros and cons, but can work if it is arranged in a careful and formal way.

The immediate advantage is that you will not have to fork out any money and might even be able to borrow the pony's tack and equipment as well. The disadvantage is that you may feel you always have someone looking over your shoulder.

Nevertheless, it can be the ideal answer for both parties, *providing* you enter into a proper, written agreement; I would get it checked by a solicitor, too (see the final chapter).

The agreement should state how long the loan period is going to be and what period of notice must be given if either side wants to withdraw from it. The pony's owner will undoubtedly want a stipulation that he or she can take the animal back if you do not keep him to the agreed standard, and will also want regular access.

It is also important to define who pays for what. Obviously you will be responsible for the day to day running costs, but what about insurance and vaccinations? You might expect these costs to be down to you, but make sure the money situation is fully understood by both sides.

Do make sure that if you have a pony on loan, your daughter understands what it means. I remember a friend's daughter who had been loaned a Dartmoor for a year howling her head off because the owner's children had criticised her at a gymkhana. They did not think she rode their pony well enough – though both he and she were perfectly happy – and made a point of telling her.

If a loan works out particularly well you might find that the owners are prepared to sell the pony to you after all. Once he is actually in someone else's care and the blow of his leaving has softened, children often find it easier to 'let go' of an old friend, particularly if a new and more exciting mount has taken his place.

4 Buying the Pony

Asking the right questions and doing a bit of detective work as described in the previous chapter should soon give you a shortlist of ponies. You might be lucky and find that the first one you look at is ideal, but it is more likely you will look at a few before making your choice.

I have always found that first impressions are important. If the pony strikes you as a confident, friendly sort of chap and comes to say hello, that is a good

A friendly sort of chap

start. If he looks apathetic and uninterested, or lays his ears back and tries to nip, things do not look so good.

Take a note of his general condition. A pony that lives out cannot possibly look as smart as his stabled, rugged-up companion, but he should still be well-covered without being fat. If it is summer, he will look reasonably sleek; if he has his winter coat on he will probably look like a teddy bear. Ask to see some recent pictures of him looking his best – it could be a surprising 'before and after'!

Conformation

When buying a first pony it is definitely a case of handsome is as handsome does. Even so, it helps to have an idea in your mind as to the ideal conformation, i.e. make and shape. These guidelines are not just someone's idea of what looks pretty, but ones that will show how a pony with good conformation is less likely to go lame and can stand up to work. You will not find one with perfect conformation (or if you do, it will have a price tag with lots of noughts on the end) but you will know what to look for. At first one pony will look much the same as another, but getting 'an eye for a horse' takes practice. Practising is in fact a good idea; try assessing the ponies at your daughter's riding school and then ask someone knowledgeable to give you their opinion.

Ask to see the pony standing square (i.e. with his weight distributed evenly over all four legs) on a level piece of ground, then stand back and gauge his proportions. Ideally his body (excluding the head and neck) should fill a square, so if you drew one round him everything would be in more or less the same proportion. Then start at the front and work your way back.

Just as we do not all have pretty or handsome faces, so ponies do not all have pretty heads – though if he has some Welsh or Dartmoor in him he is likely to have an attractive one. Do not be carried away by long eyelashes and liquid eyes; as a well-known show-jumper once remarked, a pretty head is no use unless it has a brain inside it and four good legs underneath it.

Big ears are supposed to be a sign of a generous nature, and small, piggy eyes are supposed to indicate a doubtful temperament. Maybe it is true, maybe it is not; unattractive ponies, like unattractive people, are sometimes unfairly labelled. Look for a calm eye and a pair of pricked ears and you should be all right.

When assessing conformation it is important to look at how one part fits on to the next. The head should join the neck cleanly and preferably without a too thick jowl so the pony can flex easily. The neck is equally important; one that

Ideally his body should fill a square

is too short leads to the pony holding its head too high and giving the rider the uncomfortable feeling that there is not quite enough in front of her. It also means that the pony is likely to be stiff and rigid in his movement, as he finds it difficult to make a nice round shape.

They say you should not look a gift horse in the mouth, the reason being, of course, that you can tell his age by the appearance of his teeth. It is not something you can learn in five minutes, and in any case it is hard to be accurate after ten years of age. So leave ageing the pony to your expert and the vet.

The shape of the shoulder influences the way the pony moves and therefore the sort of ride he is going to give. Some ponies have short, straight shoulders; this gives them lots of pulling power, ideal in a driving animal, but a riding animal should have a long, sloping shoulder to allow freedom of movement.

If the pony's back is too long or too short he will not fit in to your imaginary square. A long back is a weak one, though it is accepted that mares generally have longer backs than geldings. The back should lead to nicely rounded hind-quarters which is where the pony's engine is, so avoid an animal that is weak behind the saddle.

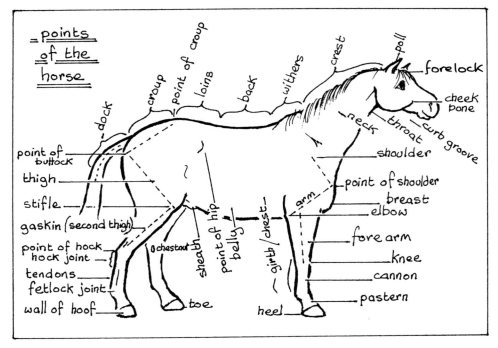

Now we come on to feet and legs, and you will soon get fed up with every-one quoting the old saying 'No foot, no horse' to you. Nevertheless, it is true. The feet are the pony's base, so first make sure they are symmetrical and thus share the weight and strain equally. Avoid weak, crumbling hooves, because it is difficult to keep shoes on them.

When picking up a pony's foot you will see a V-shaped piece at the heel end; this is called the frog and acts as a shock absorber. It should therefore be well defined and with no ragged edges; if there is a nasty smell, the pony has a disease called thrush. It can be cured, but it is a nuisance.

Where is the hock?

A pony's legs take an awful lot of strain, especially when jumping. His front legs should have flat knees, broad fetlocks, short cannon bones and pasterns that are not too upright. If all this sounds like double Dutch, check with the 'points of the horse' chart. Questions like 'What's the stifle?' and 'Where's the hock?' can keep the whole family amused for hours!

The hind legs provide the propulsion. Pay careful attention to the hocks, which are the hardest worked joints in the pony's body. They should be parallel when viewed from behind. The pony should not be sickle-hocked or cow-hocked and there should not be any swellings or puffiness. Capped hocks, which occur when a pony bangs the point of his hock – often when he has insufficient bedding – are unsightly, but do not usually cause trouble. Disfigurements like curbs and thoroughpins, swellings which an experienced person will point out to you, are a sign of weakness.

The perfect pony never has any blemishes, but real ones do unfortunately. If you find a pony with 'clean legs', that is legs without any lumps or bumps, then either you are very lucky or he has never done a day's work in his life. The most common lumps are splints, bony enlargements usually on the inside of the front legs; once formed, they rarely cause any problems, but your vet will advise you on this when he makes his inspection.

If you still like what you see, ask to see the pony trotted up in hand, but if

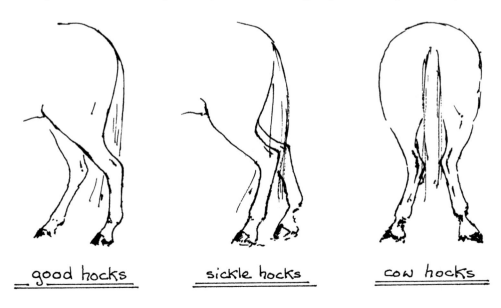

good hocks   sickle hocks   cow hocks

you have already decided that he is not the one for you, perhaps because he seems too nervous or sensitive, then now is the time to say so politely and avoid wasting everybody's time.

Seeing a pony led out in hand (in a headcollar on a long lead rope so that his movement is as natural and unrestricted as possible) tells you not only whether he is likely to be comfortable to ride, but also if he has a tendency to hurt himself by knocking one leg against the other.

Find a level piece of ground and ask to see the pony walked straight towards you, then past you and away. The handler should then turn him round and trot back, past and away from you, repeating the process if necessary so you can see how he places his front and hind legs.

The ideal pony 'moves straight', or in other words does not twist his feet in or out. His movement should be as straight as possible, but slight variations do not usually matter; your vet will tell you if there is anything to worry about. The most common variation is dishing, where the pony throws out one or both front feet. If it is pronounced, it might make him an uncomfortable ride, but many ponies dish slightly to no ill effect. Most people agree that dishing is less of a fault than plaiting, where the pony turns his hooves in, and can literally fall over his own feet. Acquiring an eye for movement is again something that comes with practice. Try whiling away your daughter's next lesson by studying the ponies on the ride when they work in trot.

Watching the Pony Work Under Saddle

The next stage is to ask to see the pony ridden by his present young owner. There are two main reasons for this – if he is going to do anything naughty, it is better he does it with a child who is used to him, and it gives you the chance to see how he behaves with a rider on his back. It also gives the sellers a chance to show him off to his best advantage.

Some people have facilities like outdoor schooling arenas or even indoor schools, but most have to make do with a simple field. In some ways the latter is better, because if he will work nicely in his field he will work nicely anywhere.

His present young rider should be able to tack him up by herself. Most ponies will puff themselves out when their girths are being tightened, but you do not want one that kicks or throws its head in the air and refuses to be bridled. If a pony objects to being tacked up it is usually because he has been roughly treated: if someone banged a metal bit against your teeth or pulled a strap tight round your stomach you would object, too!

As you watch the pony walked, trotted and cantered under saddle see how he and his rider react to each other. Is the impression a harmonious one, or is there a lot of kicking and yanking going on? Is he happy to work on either rein (that is, circling to the left and to the right) or does he seem uncomfortable on one of them? Will he go away from the gate happily, or is he always hanging towards it and trying to duck towards home? If he does the latter he is said to be napping; nappiness can be cured by a strong, capable rider, but if a pony has a nappy streak in him it will come out at some time or other.

If the partnership seems like a happy one, ask to see the pony jumped over a small fence. A cross pole with a rail behind it about eighteen inches to two foot high is perfectly adequate; ideally the pony should approach it calmly, pop over it and be easy to control afterwards. Ask to see him jump it going away from home as well as coming towards it.

By now your daughter will probably be longing to try him. She will also be a bit nervous of riding in front of strangers, so let her walk the pony round to get the feel of him and ask for trot when she is ready. Only if she is happy should they go on to canter, perhaps ending by doing a tiny jump.

As it is inevitable that your daughter will be riding out, it is important to see how a horse or pony behaves on the roads. If the owners have another pony they may offer to let her go for a short accompanied hack; if not, they should be prepared to hack him out while you follow on foot or in the car. Do not be offended if they will not let your daughter ride out alone – I would never let a total stranger go off on my horse, no matter how well behaved the animal.

Watching a pony on the roads lets you see how he reacts not only to traffic but also to 'hazards' like plastic bags and sudden noises. There is no such thing as a 'bomb-proof' pony, no matter what the advertisements say, but you do want one that is sensible under ordinary circumstances.

If the pony is taken out in company, see how he behaves when he is first behind and then in front of his companion, both going away from and coming back towards home. Will he trot away while the other pony stays in walk, and will he stay calm while the other pony trots away from him? When they get back, will he walk obediently past and away from his own gateway, or does he duck into it or refuse to go past?

All this may sound as if you are trying to set traps. In a way, you are, because if a pony has habits your daughter cannot cope with it is better to find out before handing over your money, and by trying him in different situations, you can get an idea of his temperament and outlook on life.

By now you will have a pretty good idea of whether or not your daughter and the pony are going to suit each other. However, no matter how enthusiastic she is, do give yourselves time to think about it and, if appropriate, bring your friendly expert along for a second opinion. The owners may tell you that someone else is coming to look at him later that day; it could well be true, or it might be a sales tactic, which is understandable; you will probably try it yourself one day.

It is a lot easier to find another pony than it is to sell one bought in haste and which turns out to be unsuitable. Tell the sellers you are very interested, by all means, but explain that you want to make sure your daughter and their pony are right for one another. If they are equally concerned about him getting the right home, they will understand.

If you have a knowledgeable person waiting in the wings, take them to look at the pony as soon as possible. Providing they share your opinion and do not find the pony unsound, it is now time to talk money!

Paying for the Pony

Traditionally, selling a horse involves haggling and most people are prepared to drop a little from their asking price. How much depends on what the animal is worth; a hunter advertised at £3,000 could well become yours for £2,750, but no one is going to drop £250 from the price of a £700 pony.

Usually you get what you pay for, and peace of mind is worth a great deal. If the sellers will not budge from their price, you have to respect that or find another pony. Or they may be prepared to negotiate on his tack; if it is sound and well cared for, it could be a good buy.

Once you have settled on the price, it is customary to pay a deposit subject to a satisfactory report on the pony from your vet. Most people are happy with £50 (so keep the cash with you) and should give you a receipt for it. The wording should be something along the following lines:

Accepted on May 10th, 1990, from Mr Joe Bloggs of 1, Blank Street, Blanktown, £50 deposit on the 13.2 hh chestnut pony known as Ginger. This deposit is against the agreed purchase price of £700 and is returnable to Mr Bloggs should the pony fail the vetting to be arranged by him.

The deposit is little more than a sign of good faith on both sides, though it is worth doing. It means that if you change your mind the sellers keep your £50 to make up for their wasted time and possible loss of other sales. It also means, in theory, that if they accept a higher offer you can take legal action against them. In practice it would be more trouble than it is worth, but the offering and accepting of a deposit does show good intentions on both sides.

Vetting

The last and vital test of the pony is to have him inspected by a vet. It is the equivalent of putting him through an MOT test and will cost about £45–£100 depending on how far the vet has to travel and how long the vetting takes. You may get people telling you that it is a waste of money, but to my mind it is an investment. Only a vet can tell you if a pony has something wrong with, for instance, his heart or his eyes; disappointment now is better than heartbreak later on.

A vetting is not a guarantee that the pony will not have things wrong with him later on. A veterinary certificate indicates that, in the vet's opinion, the pony was sound for your purpose on the day he examined him. That said, do not be tempted to buy without one.

These days more and more vets specialise, and one who deals with small animals might not want to undertake a horse vetting. The best way to find a vet is by asking at your daughter's riding school; the only problem you might come across is if the one who is recommended to you also acts for the people who are selling the pony. In this case, he might not feel happy doing the vetting – it is up to the individual. If he does not want to do it himself he may recommend a colleague or a vet from another practice. He will also advise you on whether you should have the full vetting, which is more expensive, or whether the shorter one will be sufficient. In the case of expensive performance animals a full vetting is essential, but in your case the vet may suggest opting for the short form and only carry out the ridden part if he has any doubts.

Ideally you should be there when the vetting is carried out, as it is much easier for the vet to explain things to you. In any case, watching a pony being vetted is very interesting, and there is plenty to learn.

The vet will start by seeing the pony in his stable or field so he is relaxed. There he will use a stethoscope to examine his heart and lungs, and will also check his eyes with an instrument called an ophthalmoscope.

By examining the pony's teeth the vet can tell you how old the animal is. He will also check for any defects, for instance an uneven bite that could cause eating problems. Then the manipulation starts, working from front to back. This enables the vet to check that muscles, joints and tendons are undamaged and working properly.

The next stage is usually to have the pony run up in hand to check his action and detect any signs of lameness. If you are having a full vetting the vet will then want to see the pony ridden by the seller. This will include a period of fast work after which he will listen to his breathing for signs of abnormality.

The flexion or spavin test is usually carried out in both forms of vetting, always on the hind legs and sometimes on the forelegs as well. The vet holds up the pony's leg for a short while and then, immediately the leg is released, has him trotted forwards. Any unevenness of gait signifies a problem. He will ask for the pony to be turned sharply in tight circles to check that he can cross his hind legs, and will also ask him to be walked backwards for a few strides. Finally, he will examine the pony's feet and test their response to pressure before giving you his verdict.

There is no such thing as the perfect horse, and the vet will take this into account. He will tell you whether or not he thinks the pony will be sound and suitable for your purpose – and there is nothing like a vet's opinion to give you peace of mind!

5 Saddlery and Tack

Saddlers' shops are irresistable places, full of fascinating bits and pieces and with that lovely smell of leather in the air. Now you have a pony in the family you will quickly become familiar with them; so will your cheque book, though the good news is that major purchases like saddles last for years.

Most of the shopping can be done when you have actually got the pony home, but some things need to be bought in advance. If you are lucky, you might get the chance to buy good quality, well cared for tack with him. Ask your expert to check it over, because worn or badly fitting tack is dangerous. Amazingly, there are a lot of otherwise knowledgeable people who think it does not matter if a bit is slightly too large or too small or if a saddle is not quite right.

As a general guide, look for any signs of stress or wear in leather and stitching. Obviously ordinary use will cause wear, but it should not be excessive. Check parts where metal rubs against leather, for instance where the reins and bridle fasten on to the bit and where the stirrup leathers slot through the irons.

Other potential danger areas are those where leather and stitching comes in contact with a sweaty pony; on the girth for example. Do not be frightened to get hold of reins and stirrup leathers and give them a good tug – it might be a bit embarrassing if they fall to pieces in your hands, but think how much worse it would be if they broke and resulted in your daughter falling off on the road.

If you are working to a tight budget, ask your riding school to recommend a good local saddler and ask them about buying second-hand tack. A good compromise is often to buy a second-hand saddle and the rest new – the new synthetic saddles can also be good alternatives. A professional saddler will help you find one that is the right size for pony and rider and is in good condition.

You might see saddlery auctions advertised in your local paper, and people who know what they are looking for can sometimes pick up bargains. Equally, they can get carried away in the excitement of bidding and either pay more than they should or buy something they do not really want! The biggest danger with sales is that you sometimes find cheap leather goods from the Far East. The bridles might look nice, but the leather is weak and inevitably dangerous.

Here, then, is a guide to your pony's basic wardrobe. These are the basic essentials – luxuries like travelling equipment can come later.

Headcollar and Lead Rope

These are used for occasions when you need to control the pony but do not need to use a bridle. For instance, he will wear his headcollar when you are leading him to and from the field or tying him up to groom him. If, however, you are leading a pony along the road he should wear his bridle, for safety's sake. The quietest pony can spook at the unexpected, and in these circumstances a bridle gives more control.

Ordinary, everyday headcollars are made from nylon web. Cheap, cheerful and available in lots of colours, they are virtually unbreakable. For this reason, it is not advisable to leave one on a pony when he is turned out. If he hooks it over something and gets caught, he is likely to pull back in panic and could hurt himself or even break his neck. If he is sometimes hard to catch and you feel you must leave a headcollar on, buy a chrome leather one; leather will snap in an emergency, which is better than the pony getting hurt.

As your daughter progresses and you think about going to shows, you will want a proper leather headcollar for best. Some have brass fittings and even a little brass nameplate engraved with the pony's name. This, however, goes on the luxury list. Thinking of Christmas and birthday presents is never a problem with a pony in the family.

Headcollars come in either small, medium or large or pony, cob and full size. A pony with a big head might need a cob size one. It should be fitted so that the noseband comes halfway between the bottom of the cheekbones (they're easy to feel when you stroke the pony's face) and the corners of his mouth.

Lead ropes can be bought in the same colour as your nylon headcollar. Most people like to choose a colour scheme and stick to it, which is why you will see lots of smart little ponies in matching headcollars, ropes, rugs and travelling gear. The commonest kind of lead rope has a clip on the end similar to those on dog leads; make sure it is clipped on to the headcollar so that the end cannot dig

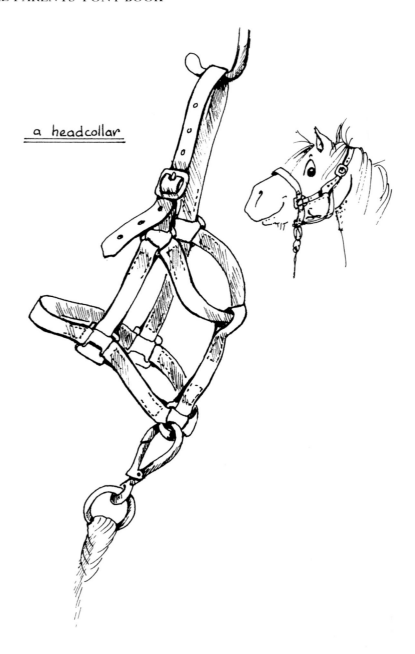

a headcollar

in to the pony. Headcollar ropes always break or go missing when you need them, so it is a good idea to keep a spare one handy.

Saddles

The saddle is the biggest single purchase you will have to make, apart from the pony, so expert advice is vital.

The saddle must fit both pony and rider, and while you can learn to make a rough assessment it really takes a proper saddler to make the final judgement. An ill-fitting saddle can, at worst, damage your pony's back, and will certainly make him unhappy and badly behaved. How would you feel if you were expected to work in a pair of shoes that were the wrong size?

There are lots of specialist saddles for specialist purposes, from tiny, light-weight racing ones to those for dressage and jumping. Your daughter will need a general purpose saddle, which, as its name suggests, is suitable for most activities at an ordinary level. If she will be coping with tacking up on her own much of the time, one of the new generation of synthetic saddles could be worth looking at. They are light, hard-wearing and easy to clean. The early versions were not particularly good-looking, but the latest models have improved beyond recognition.

Ponies, like people, come in all shapes and sizes. Some are narrow, others decidedly more rotund. Some have high withers while in others they are less pronounced. If you tell your saddler the height of your pony and what type he is, he will take your daughter's height and build into consideration and be able to bring out a selection of saddles to try on the pony. Your daughter will be able to ride in them, and the saddler will recommend the best one. Sometimes it is a matter of compromise, but the pony's comfort must always come first.

Never buy a saddle without having it tried on the pony and ridden on. It must not pinch the pony or move about too much (though some movement is inevitable) and when the rider is mounted there should always be a clear channel visible along the gullet from front to back. If you stand in front of or behind the pony, you should see daylight through the saddle gullet with a rider on board. There should be a three-finger width space between the front arch of the saddle (the pommel) and the withers, and the top of the gullet at the back of the saddle and the pony's back. Finally, check that the pony's shoulders are unrestricted when he is moving and that the saddle is not pinching there – then ask your saddler to make sure. He can improve the fit by reshaping the saddle's stuffing, but he cannot make a silk purse out of a sow's ear.

New saddles take a little time to settle, and need reflocking (to have the

Parts of the saddle

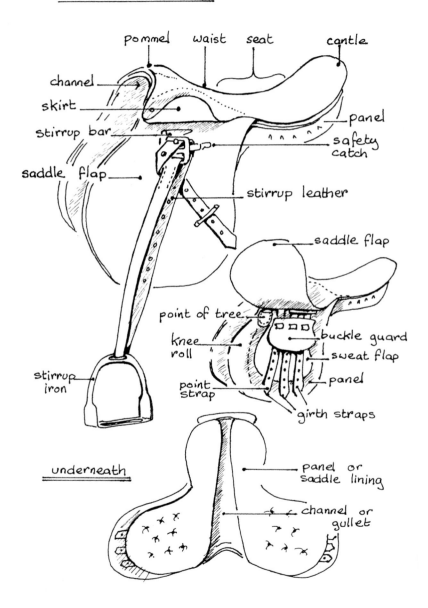

pommel   waist   seat   cantle

channel

skirt

stirrup bar

saddle flap

panel

safety catch

stirrup leather

saddle flap

point of tree

knee roll

buckle guard

sweat flap

panel

point strap

girth straps

stirrup iron

underneath

panel or saddle lining

channel or gullet

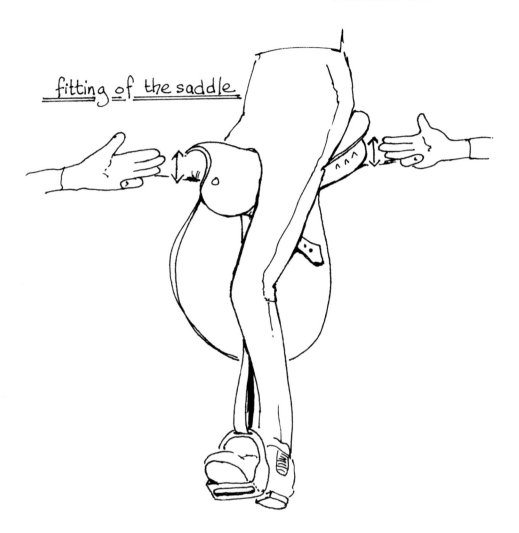

fitting of the saddle

stuffing adjusted) from time to time. The first reflock may be free, but this is up to the individual saddler, and subsequently may only cost a few pounds. If there is any sign of pinching or rubbing do check with your saddler.

To go with your saddle you will need stirrup irons and leathers, a girth and a couple of numnahs (pads which are the same shape as the saddle and go underneath it).

STIRRUPS

Stirrup irons should always be made of stainless steel and should be an inch wider than the widest part of the rider's boot. If they are too small or too big it is possible that her foot could get trapped in a fall, with horrifying consequences. The best stirrup leathers are rawhide. They come in different lengths, so ask your saddler to help you find the right length. Stirrup treads (ridged rubber pads which slip into the bottom of the iron) are universally used and accepted, and help to stop the feet slipping.

Safety stirrups are a good idea for children; the strong rubber band, which must be positioned to the outside, will come off if the rider falls, and prevent the foot from being trapped. (left) 'closed' stirrup with band in place, (right) 'open' stirrup without band

GIRTHS

There are many different kinds of girth, some more expensive than others and each with its own advantages and disadvantages. My own preference is for a leather girth, provided it is kept clean and supple, or for one of the padded cotton-mix types. The latter are cheaper than leather, can be washed in the washing machine and absorb sweat to a certain extent.

Girths come in different lengths, so if you describe your pony's height and build, your saddler will help you choose. The girth should be tight enough to

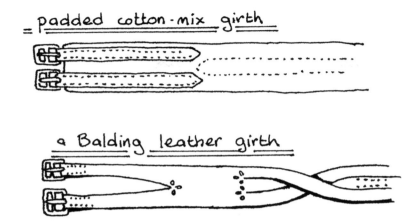

= padded cotton-mix girth

a Balding leather girth

prevent the saddle from slipping and should always be checked before the rider gets on and after they have ridden for a few minutes. Many ponies blow their stomachs out when the girth is fastened, and it can be a shock to find that you can suddenly slip your arm between it and his belly! To ensure the girth is not pinching him, pull each of the pony's forelegs forward in turn before he is mounted; if the skin is pinched into folds, nasty sores called girth galls can be caused. It is a good idea to have two girths, and two numnahs.

NUMNAHS
Numnahs can be made from a variety of materials, including expensive sheepskin, but, for easy care, the quilted cotton kind that wash well are best – a dirty, sweaty numnah can cause skin problems. Make sure that, when saddling up, the numnah is pulled well into into the saddle gullet and not pressing down on the pony's spine.

Bridles, Bits and Bitting

A basic bridle consists of a headpiece, browband, cheekstraps, some kind of noseband, reins and bit. There are two main categories of bit; the snaffle and the curb, but there are many different kinds of bit within those categories. The snaffle and the curb differ in how they give instruction to the horse, and the type of instructions given.

The snaffle operates on the corner of the mouth by direct rein action, the reins attaching to rings at the corners of the mouth. The curb has long cheeks –

You can slip an arm between the girth and the belly

the reins attach to the bottom of the cheeks – and is always used with a curb chain which sits lightly in the horse's chin groove. The combination of long cheeks and curb chain gives the bit a leverage action.

The bit combined with parts of the bridle working on certain pressure points on the horse's head, plus the rider's aids, all contribute to the control of the horse.

You may see horses at shows wearing two bits at once. This is a double bridle and consists of a small-ringed, fine snaffle, called a bridoon, and a curb bit. Double bridles should only be used by experienced riders on well-schooled horses, and allow for very sensitive, accurate communication.

parts of the bridle

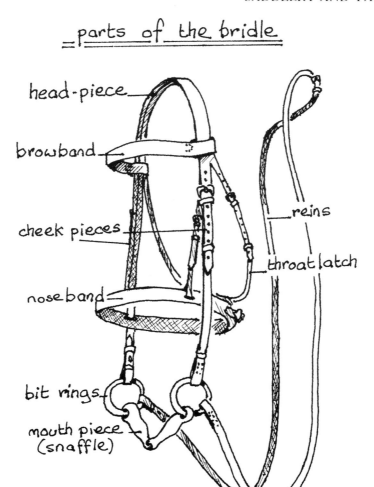

head-piece

browband

cheek pieces

noseband

bit rings

mouth piece
(snaffle)

reins

throat latch

A first pony should go well in some kind of snaffle, and when you buy your pony he should already be working happily with the bit he has, so the sensible thing is to stick to that bit unless your instructor advises you otherwise.

It is important that a bit is the right width for the pony and is neither too high nor too low in his mouth. There should be about a quarter of an inch of mouth-

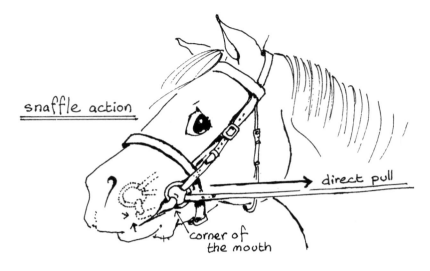

snaffle action

direct pull

corner of
the mouth

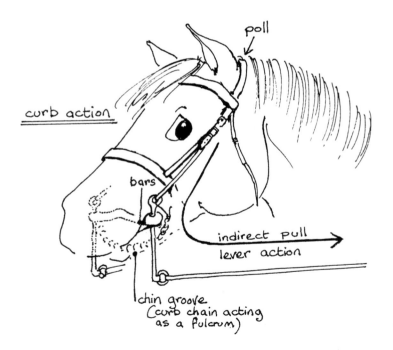

poll

curb action

bars

indirect pull
lever action

chin groove
(curb chain acting
as a fulcrum)

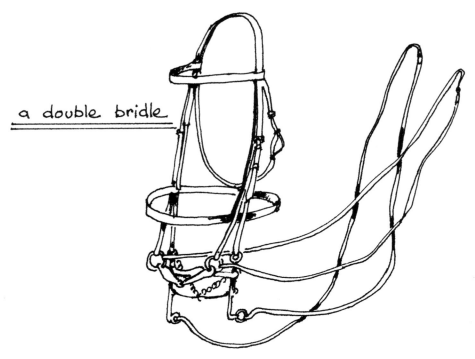

a double bridle

piece on each side between the bit rings (or the cheeks of a cheek snaffle or curb bit) and his lips, and it should be high enough to just wrinkle the corners of his mouth. If the bit is too low it will bang against the pony's teeth, and he may also be able to get his tongue over the bit.

Bitting is a fascinating and complicated subject, but think in terms of the simpler the better and you will not go far wrong. Some people think that if a pony is strong the answer is to put a more severe bit in his mouth, but sometimes this can make matters worse. A pony's natural reaction is to run away from anything that frightens or hurts him, so a strong bit can sometimes make him pull more. This problem is dealt with in more detail in a later chapter, but for the moment stick to the snaffle, and ask your instructor's advice if you run into problems.

SNAFFLES
A snaffle bit can have a straight, half-moon, single- or double-jointed mouthpiece. The mouthpiece is usually metal (and in this case should always be made from stainless steel) but it can also be covered in rubber or made from

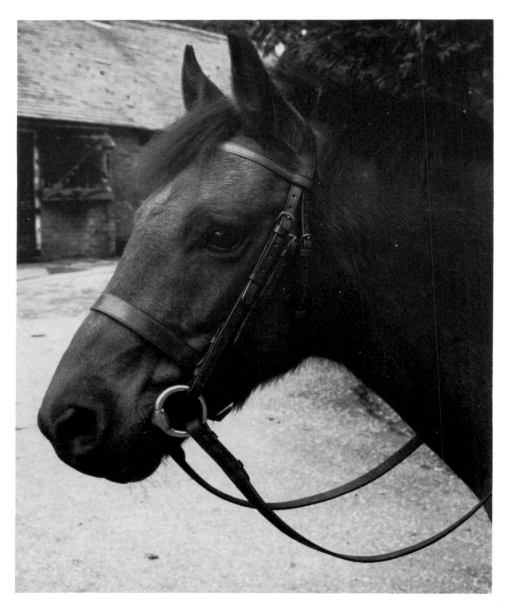

A correctly fitted snaffle bridle with cavesson noseband and eggbutt snaffle

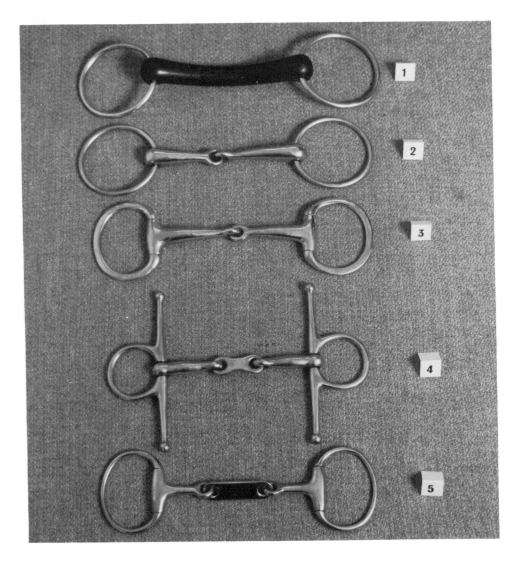

Types of bit: 1) loose-ring vulcanite snaffle; 2) loose-ring jointed snaffle; 3) jointed eggbutt snaffle. These three are mild bits as is 4) a French link snaffle, but it must not be confused with 5) a Dr Bristol. The Dr Bristol, which has a central plate with flat sides as opposed to the kidney-shaped plate of the French link snaffle, is a more severe bit suitable only for an experienced rider

vulcanised (specially hardened) rubber. Whatever kind your pony wears it is vital that it fits properly, that there are no sharp edges and that it is kept clean. As a general rule, the thicker the mouthpiece the kinder the action of the bit, though any bit can only be as kind as the hands at the end of the reins.

At the ends of the mouthpiece you will find the rings to which the reins are attached. The rings can be different shapes depending on what action is needed. The commonest is the eggbutt snaffle, which cannot pinch the pony's mouth, but he may wear a loose-ring snaffle which allows him to play with the bit more. Another variation is some kind of cheek snaffle, which can help with steering and is often used on young horses. The full cheeks press against the side of the animal's face.

Some ponies do not like the single-jointed snaffle, which has a nutcracker action, and are happier with a half-moon mouthpiece or a French snaffle. The latter has a kidney shaped piece in the middle that removes the nutcracker action; if your pony wears one of these and you buy a new one, be sure not to confuse it with the similar looking but more severe Dr Bristol bit. A Dr Bristol also has a centre piece, but it has flat sides and puts pressure on the tongue.

PELHAMS AND CURBS

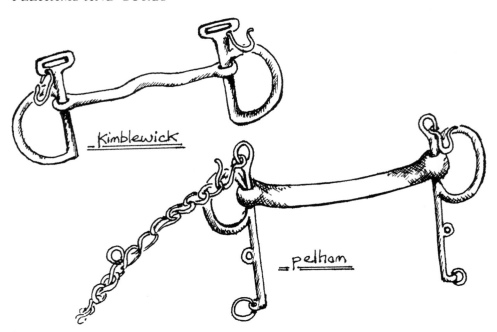

Kimblewick

pelham

There is also a bit called a pelham which attempts to combine the action of a bridoon and curb in one bit. In theory it does not work, but in practice some ponies go very well in one. If used carefully the thick mouthpiece is a kind one, and it can give greater control over a pony who gets strong in exciting situations like cross-country. A pelham can be used with two pairs of reins or with one rein joined to a leather coupling.

A kimblewick, another kind of curb bit not suitable for novice riders, has one ring at each end of the mouthpiece and one pair of reins. Neither should be needed for your first pony, but it is interesting to look at all the different bits that are available.

NOSEBANDS

The simplest form of noseband, the cavesson, is really only of cosmetic value. It makes the horse's head look more attractive, as you will see if you compare pictures of racehorses without nosebands and other horses with them. Having said that, a cavesson noseband fitted *slightly* tighter and lower than normal can discourage a pony from opening his mouth too much.

The cavesson noseband, like the one on your headcollar, should come half-way between the bottom of the pony's cheekbones and the corners of his mouth. You should buckle it just tight enough to allow two fingers to slip between it and his nose when your hand is held flat against his face.

Some horses and ponies learn to open their mouths to evade the action of the

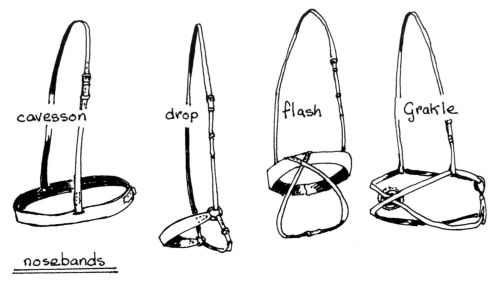

cavesson   drop   flash   Grakle

nosebands

bit. Usually the fault lies at some stage with a rider who has been un-sympathetic with their hands, and tactful but firm riding can ease the problem. To give more control, though, it is sometimes best to fit some kind of drop noseband – as long as you bear in mind that you are not using it to strap the pony's mouth shut and that you must always take care to ensure that it does not interfere with his breathing.

The simple drop noseband goes lower than the cavesson and buckles below the bit. When fitting it, make sure it does not rest on the soft part of his nose; you should be able to get four fingers' width between the bottom of the noseband and the top of his nostrils. Most people fasten it slightly tighter than the cavesson, but if it is too tight it will only cause discomfort and make the problem worse.

Flash nosebands are not as definite in their action as the ordinary drop kind and for that reason some ponies are happier in them. They consist of a cavesson with a loop at the front centre, which is used to anchor a second strap which goes below the bit. A flash noseband can be used with a standing martingale (see the section on martingales) as long as the martingale is buckled to the cavesson. It should never be fastened to any kind of drop noseband, nor should a drop noseband be used with any bit other than some form of snaffle.

The disadvantage of a flash noseband is that the cavesson part can be pulled down. To avoid this, fasten it slightly tighter than normal, making sure that the pony is not being pinched or rubbed. The drop strap should be tightened so you can comfortably slip a finger between it and the pony's nose; some people buckle it on the side, but I prefer to fasten it so the buckle is below that of the cavesson and it cannot rub or pinch the soft part of the nose.

The third kind of noseband is the Grackle or crossover kind. It gets its name from the racehorse for whom it was invented, who pulled like a train! It is a popular noseband with event riders, who need to control fit horses at speed across country, but you should not need one on a first pony.

BROWBAND AND THROATLATCH

Both the browband and the throatlatch are there to keep the bridle in place, but neither must be too tight. Browbands are not adjustable, but come in different widths, so make sure yours does not pinch the pony's ears. Plain leather ones are neat and tidy, but some people like brass studded or coloured ones. The throatlatch should be fastened so you can get a hand's width between it and the pony's face; many people fasten them too tight.

Browband and throatlatch; neither must be too tight

REINS

Reins can be made from many kinds of material. Plain leather ones are fine, but most people prefer rubber covered ones or the Continental web kind with leather handstops. The reason is that they give a better grip in wet weather; plain leather becomes slippery and inevitably you have less control. Whatever sort you choose, do not pick ones that are too wide or narrow for your daughter's hands.

Martingales

In theory every pony should go quietly and obediently in a simple snaffle bridle with a cavesson noseband. In practice some riders find they need a bit of extra help, usually in the form of a martingale. Do not let your daughter fit one because she thinks it looks smart, or because her friend's pony wears one, but if your riding instructor says it would be a good idea ask her advice on type and fitting.

The two commonest kinds are the standing and running martingales, both designed to give the rider more control over the way the pony carries his head. Both start off as a strap which fastens to the girth and runs through a neckstrap; the standing martingale is buckled to a cavesson noseband (or the cavesson part of a flash) while the running martingale splits into two straps. Each has a small ring at the end through which the reins are passed.

Standing martingales were unfashionable at one time, but now they are coming back into favour again. If a pony raises his head too high it puts pressure on the noseband, thus, in theory, persuading him to lower his head. The advantage is that it does not interfere with the reins, and the disadvantage is that if fastened too tightly it can interfere with the pony's freedom to stretch his head and neck, especially when jumping.

The running martingale keeps the bit in position when the pony puts his head too high, but if it is too tight the pressure on the reins puts constant pressure on the pony's mouth and interferes with the rider's signals. Do not look on it as a sign of abject failure if your pony wears a martingale, but do get an expert to fit it and aim to school him so that eventually he does not need it, except perhaps for jumping.

If your pony does not need a martingale, a neckstrap can still be a good idea. It is far better to grab a neckstrap if you lose your balance than to pull the pony in the mouth. Your saddler will either make you one that fastens to the rings at the front of the saddle with two smaller straps (the best and most secure kind, as it will not slip down the pony's neck) or you can improvise with a spare stirrup leather.

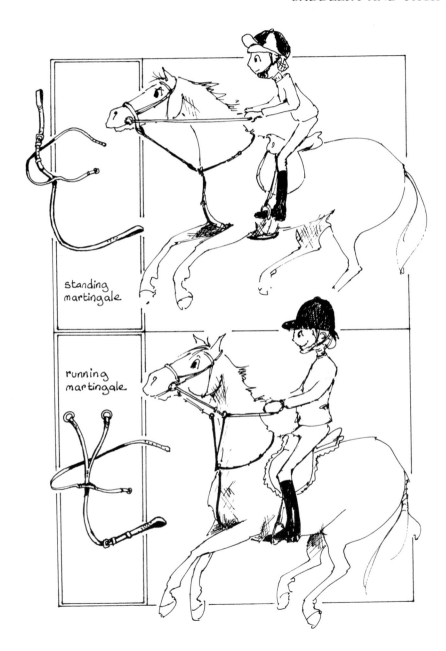

standing
martingale

running
martingale

Rugs

If your pony is living out all or most of the time he will almost certainly need a New Zealand rug to keep him warm and dry in bad winter weather – preferably two, so he has a spare in case the other gets wet inside or ripped. The only ponies who are the exception to this rule are some native ponies whose own winter coats are so dense that they fluff out and keep the pony better protected than any rug could.

If he is going to be stabled at night he will also need some kind of stable rug. A sweat rug is useful, too. To find out what size rug he needs, measure from the centre of his chest to a point in line with his tail setting. Armed with that information and a description of his type, your saddler will steer you towards the best makes of rugs.

A properly fitting New Zealand rug. These rugs are fastened either by a surcingle, cross surcingles, legstraps, or a combination of these fastenings

NEW ZEALAND RUGS

These range from the cheap and cheerful to the luxurious. For the pony who lives out, proper protection is a must. You get what you pay for, and cheap rugs usually do not fit or wear as well. In the long run, a good but perhaps more expensive rug is more cost effective than a barely adequate cheap one.

Materials range from cotton canvas to lightweight, 'breathable' fabrics. Some have to be reproofed regularly; you can ask your saddler to do this for you or buy reproofer from him to do it yourself.

A New Zealand rug (which not surprisingly takes its name from its country of origin) has to fit well and stay in place. Many ponies enjoy nothing better than an energetic roll, and a rug that slips will not only leave him unprotected but can also make him sore by rubbing and chafing.

The old-fashioned type of rug with a surcingle (a strap buckling over the back and round the belly) is not so popular now because surcingles can put pressure on the spine. Rollers, which are surcingles with padding so there is no spine pressure, are much better – but they can still slip on an energetic pony. The best kinds of fastenings are cross surcingles, which cross under the belly; legstraps, which cross between the hind legs, or a combination of both.

STABLE RUGS

If your pony has a New Zealand on in the day he will need a stable rug at night. When he is out he can move around to find shelter and keep warm, but his freedom is obviously restricted when he is stabled.

Again, materials vary, but most people prefer some kind of washable rug. The most popular are quilted ones with some kind of tough outer covering (usually nylon) and cotton lining. Cotton is comfortable for the pony and you will not get a build-up of static. The guidelines for fastenings are the same as for New Zealands.

SWEAT RUGS

Strictly speaking, these should be called anti-sweat rugs. They look like big string vests and are used to help a sweating pony cool down without catching a chill. Unless the weather is very hot, they need to have another rug over the top of them because they work by trapping a layer of air between the two rugs.

A sweat rug is also useful for 'thatching' a wet pony. If he is wet and muddy and you want to dry him off, put a layer of clean, dry straw along his back and loins and put a sweat rug over the top. You can also use hessian sacks for thatching, if you can find them.

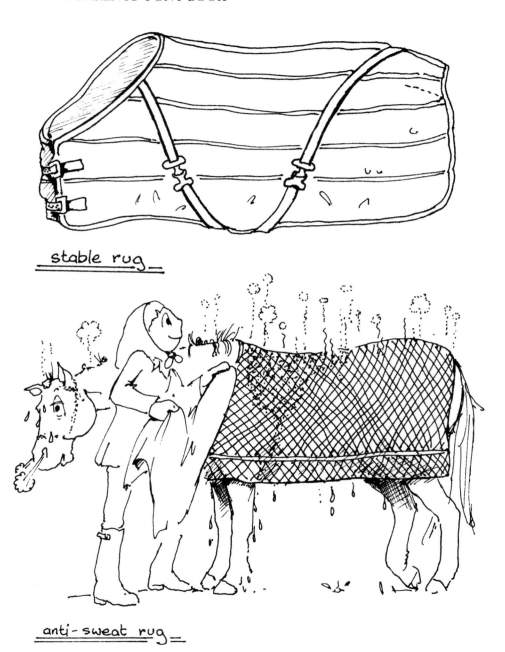

stable rug

anti-sweat rug

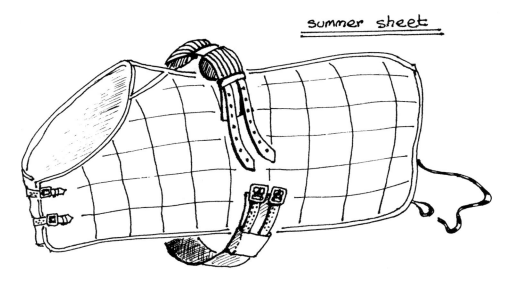

summer sheet

SUMMER SHEETS

These are cotton rugs used for travelling a pony in summer, to keep him clean if he is going to a show and sometimes to keep the flies off him. They are not essential, but can help save on washing if you put one under the pony's stable rug. It will keep the lining clean and you need only wash the summer sheet until the outside of the stable rug becomes too stained.

Care of Rugs and Tack

Tack and rugs are expensive, and the better they are looked after the longer they will last. Washable stable rugs are easy; most pony-sized ones will go in your washing machine. New Zealands can have the dried mud brushed off them and should be reproofed as, or if, necessary; some of the modern ones can be washed in cool to lukewarm water, but it is not really worth it until you are about to put them in storage for the summer.

Keep an eye on fastenings and make sure any chrome leather legstraps are kept supple. Fastening them correctly, linking one through the other between the pony's hind legs, keeps them away from his skin. Always make sure a rug is clean and dry before putting it away.

In a perfect world tack should be stripped (taken to pieces) and cleaned every time it is used. In the real world, that is not always possible – but there are some essential jobs that only take a minute or two and are vital both for the pony's comfort and his rider's safety.

Always wash the bit after use, as saliva and bits of food will dry and harden on the mouthpiece. The pony will not like it, there is a possibility it could cause infection and it could make him difficult to bridle. Clean water and an old nailbrush are the most effective combination here.

Mud should be wiped off and the saddle and bridle given a wipe over with a damp sponge. A quick application of saddle soap as you check for signs of wear and tear and it is all done. Sensible children will manage all this by themselves – but sensible parents will keep an eye on things.

At least once a week tack should be thoroughly cleaned and checked, and treated with leather dressing when needed. Ask your saddler to recommend a good brand and advise you on how often your tack will need doing.

Take the bridle to pieces and remove the girth, numnah, stirrups and leathers from the saddle. Using a sponge and warm water (cold water will not dissolve the grease from the pony's coat that transfers on to the leather) wash the tack without soaking it. Everyone has a favourite way of removing stubborn lumps of grease; the traditional method is to roll a few hairs from the pony's tail into a ball and gently scrub them off. I prefer to use an old facecloth, which is abrasive enough to be effective but doesn't damage the leather.

The next step is to rub saddle soap on a barely damp sponge – old-fashioned grooms spat on their sponges, but these days that is not really socially acceptable! If the saddle soap lathers, your sponge is too wet. Rub it on both sides of the leather, paying especial attention to the underneath, which is the absorbent side. Check for signs of wear and tear and put it all back together again. Saddle soaps come in liquid as well as solid preparations.

Do not be tempted to use shoe polish on tack. It might give a nice shine, but it also makes the leather extremely slippery.

If pony and rider get caught in a downpour, let the tack dry naturally indoors. Do not put it in front of a fire or radiator because it will go hard and be prone to cracking. Once it has dried out, apply leather dressing or oil.

Washable girths and numnahs can go in the washing machine, though girths should be tied up in an old pillowcase first to prevent the buckles catching on, and damaging, the washing machine drum. If the pony is shedding his coat, invest in one of the little rubber gadgets advertised to remove pet hairs from everything – it saves your machine getting clogged up with horsehair.

Tacking Up

Tacking up a pony (putting on his saddle and bridle) is a simple process but one that should never be rushed; take your time, make sure that he is comfortable and you should not have many problems. If, however, he learns to associate tacking up with discomfort and rough handling, he will soon object and start to play up. You should untack, i.e. unsaddle, him with equal care.

BRIDLING THE PONY

When bridling the pony, stand on his near (left) side at the side of his head – if you are left-handed, you might find it easier to work from the off (right) side, in which case you will need to reverse the lefts and rights in the following instructions.

1. Undo the pony's headcollar and fasten it around his neck to stop him walking away. Check that the throatlatch and noseband are undone. Holding the bridle in the left hand, gently place the reins over the pony's head leaving them at the top of his neck near his ears. By holding the reins under his throat, they can be used to control the pony, but leaving the headcollar round his neck until he is completely tacked up gives a little more control. Now take the bridle in your right hand, holding it halfway down the cheekpieces, and standing so that your arm is tucked under his throat rest the hand holding the bridle gently on his face to stop him throwing his head up.

2. Support the bit with your left hand and gently slip your thumb into the side of his mouth, where there is a convenient gap (the bars of the mouth where the bit rests when the pony is bridled). Some people will tell you to press down to get the pony to open his mouth, but quite a few remain oblivious to this hint. Gently tickling the tongue usually has the desired effect and you can then carefully slide the bit in.

3. Slip the headpiece into place, easing one ear at a time underneath it, and bring the forelock over the browband. Fasten the throatlatch and noseband to the correct tension, and check that the height of the noseband is correct, and that the bit is the correct width and in the right position. The correct fitting of the bridle and bit is described earlier in the chapter.

SADDLING THE PONY

Putting the saddle on should seem quite easy after the bridle!

1. Make sure that the stirrup irons are run up the leathers and the girth is folded over the seat, then stand at the pony's side, level with his withers. It

Bridling the pony

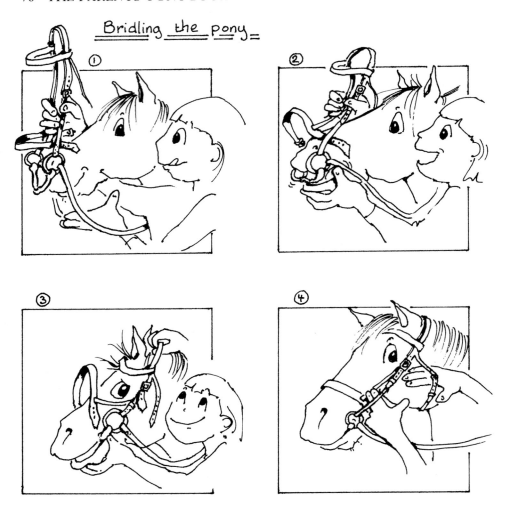

is usual to do everything from the near side, but in practical terms it is useful to accustom ponies to being handled from both sides.

2. Put the saddle down gently on the pony's back, a little too far forward at first, then slide it back into position to ensure that the hairs underneath are not caught up, and are lying flat – the same technique is used when putting on rugs. If you are using a numnah check that it too is lying flat, but pulled up into the gullet. Let the girth down carefully, so it does not bang against the pony's legs, and after checking that it is not twisted, fasten it firmly but

Saddling the pony

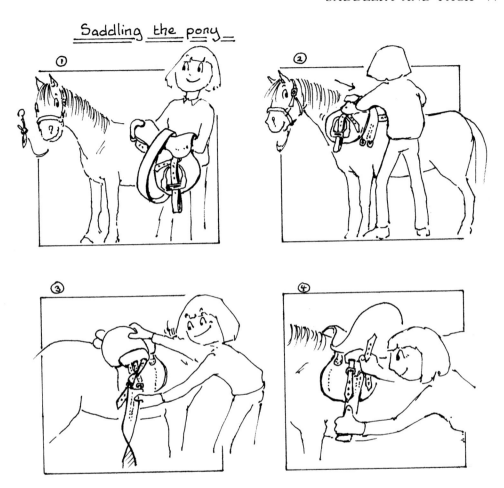

not tightly. Take it up a hole at a time until it is secure enough for mounting. Remind the rider that she will need to check it and probably tighten it again after the pony has walked on a little way.

UNTACKING

Untacking is usually done in the reverse order; saddle then bridle.

1. To unsaddle run the stirrups up the leathers, undo the girth and put it over the seat and lift the saddle off.
2. To take the bridle off, undo the noseband and throatlatch and either take

the reins over the pony's head or leave them resting on his neck depending on the circumstances. If you are untacking in the open and replacing the bridle with a headcollar you need to have some control until you have fitted the latter.

3. Take hold of the bridle headpiece and lift it gently over his ears. He will automatically drop the bit, which you should allow to slip out, taking care that it does not catch on his teeth. Some ponies grab the bit when being unbridled because they have been hurt; in this case go slowly and patiently, using the same technique to make him open his mouth as when you put the bridle on.

4. If you are putting a headcollar on, hold the bridle and reins under his throat and guide the headcollar on before taking the reins over his head. If the pony is being turned out, never slap him on the rump to encourage him to trot off – one day he will do it as soon as the bit comes out of his mouth, leaving you with a broken bridle.

6 Pony Behaviour

The average first pony should by definition be a sensible sort. With a bit of luck he will have been everywhere and done everything, so once he has settled in to his new home, life in general should hold few terrors. It is important to remember, though, that ponies are creatures of instinct and habit. In many ways predictable, they will nevertheless sometimes behave in ways that seem strange to us, and to understand why, it is necessary to look at how the horse has evolved over the years.

Camargue horses in their natural habitat in France. Horses are herd animals, and it is unfair to keep a pony or horse alone

Your pony might not look like a wild animal, but over fifty million years ago his ancestor was a browsing animal not much bigger than a large dog, with eyes in the front of his head and toes instead of hooves. Gradually he became bigger; he had three toes, but only ran on the central one, so the others disappeared as generation succeeded generation. The big changes came during the Miocene period, between 25 and 10 million years ago; jungles had evolved into plains, so in order to survive the horse had to adapt. His teeth became stronger, his neck longer and his eyes were now in the sides of his head instead of at the front.

Horses are not naturally aggressive animals, and if a horse kicks or bites it is usually in defence rather than an act of aggression. His attitude is one of 'flight not fight'; he will run away from something that frightens him rather than stand his ground and fight it. He also finds strength in numbers; in the wild he is never a solitary animal but always a member of a herd, in which he will have his own place in the pecking order.

When you look at the way horses are kept today, it is a wonder they are so accepting. It is not natural for them to be stabled except when being ridden regularly, yet many horses and ponies spend most of their time confined in a stable when their instinct is to keep moving and grazing. Your pony will be better off than many racehorses and top class competition horses, because at least he will spend most of his time living the way he was intended to.

The way you treat your pony must take his inherited characteristics into account. His eyesight is very different from ours; for example, your pony will not be able to see his own front feet, but when he is grazing he will be able to see to the sides and behind, with a 'blind spot' just ahead. He also has very sensitive hearing and a keen sense of smell, as you will find out when you are out riding – he will hear the hoofbeats of another pony long before you do, and may well be very unhappy about having to go past a herd of pigs. I once had a horse who was terrified of donkeys; he shook with fear when asked to walk past one in a field at the side of the road, and would try to whip round and canter off in the opposite direction.

Ponies hate loud noises and jerky movements, so keep your voice soft and avoid making sudden movements. When you approach a pony, whether your own or someone else's, speak to him first and try and approach him slightly from the side. If you go up to him straight-on he will not see you until the last minute, and will be startled.

If you have ever watched well-meaning people who know nothing about horses go up to one, they will often raise their hand suddenly and pat him on the nose or between the eyes. Even the quietest ponies object to this, and will

A keen sense of smell

either throw their heads up or shoot backwards in alarm. Some ponies like being fussed, others do not, and although some will stand blissfully while you gently pull their ears through your hands, others hate having their ears touched at all.

A firm pat on the neck is generally regarded as a sign of approval, and can help to relax a tense horse. Your pony will let you know what he does and does not like, so learn to read the signals. Does he push his nose at you for attention, or does he move away or even lay his ears back when you pet him a lot? If he tends to be aloof, do not irritate him by stroking or fussing him.

If you watch two horses turned out in a field together, you might see them enjoying some 'mutual grooming', gently nagging with their teeth at a spot at the base of the neck, in front of the withers. If you firmly massage that spot with your fingers, your pony will often enjoy it. Be careful, though, that he does not instinctively repay the favour by nibbling you in return!

There are times when your pony deserves his peace and quiet, for instance if he is brought into his stable for a feed. Even if you are in a hurry, it is not fair to mess around with him while he is eating. Save grooming for later, when he has finished, and let him eat at his own pace. Ponies can be irritable when they are eating, and while bad manners should never be tolerated you cannot blame him for laying his ears back if you want to plait his mane while he is eating his breakfast.

Opinions vary as to horses' intelligence. Some people swear that their ponies can do all sorts of clever things, but a lot of that is wishful thinking on the part of proud owners. Horses and ponies are not stupid, but nor do they have the intelligence of a dog – the latter, after all, has shared our home for thousands of years. Interestingly, Arab horses are often said to be more intelligent than other breeds, because in their natural habitat they live much closer to their owners.

Ponies are instinctive, not logical. Your pony will not love you for yourself, but he will be happy with you if you treat him fairly and consistently. It is very flattering when he whinnies as he sees you and comes trotting to the fence, but he is probably thinking 'Here comes food'. In the wild, he would learn his place in the herd and be quite happy sticking to it. That is exactly the situation you have to achieve in your relationship – he must be happy to accept you as his 'herd leader' without being frightened of you.

When we train a horse, we do it in the form of reward and punishment. That does not mean stuffing him with food when he does what we want and hitting him when he does not. When you are riding him and he works hard and well, it is a reward to let him have a rest. Similarly, if he tries to bite you when you are doing the girth up, scold him . . . as long as you are sure that you are not causing him discomfort by being rough.

Consistency is everything. It is no good laughing when he shies at something and you are in a good mood, only to hit him for doing it the next day because something has gone wrong and you are in a bad temper. Never punish a pony for being frightened, because you will only reinforce the fear. Be firm, insist that he does what you have asked him to do and reward him when he does it. Both rewards and punishments should immediately follow the incident that prompted them. There's no earthly use in smacking a pony two minutes after he's bitten you – he should get one short, sharp slap straight away.

If you do have to hit a pony, do it immediately and do it once only. Some people say that a pony who bites should be slapped on the nose, but this can help to make him head shy and he will probably just bite and then jerk his head away. The best place is just behind the girth, where the rider's legs are used.

Ponies, like children, can be naughty, and, like children, if they are allowed to get away with it they will push their advantage next time. You have to learn to tell the difference between a naughty pony and a frightened one. If you are asking him to do something new, he might find it a bit worrying at first; keep calm and keep insisting and you should win. If you do not, get some expert help.

The calmer you stay, the calmer your pony will remain. A tense rider or handler makes a tense pony, so take some deep breaths, give him a reassuring pat and talk to him! It does not really matter what you say – sing nursery rhymes to him if you like. But remember that ponies love being talked to and your voice is an important aid. Low, soothing tones have a calming effect and injecting a bit of encouragement into your voice can also have a remarkable effect.

When you are handling a pony, whether you are leading him or brushing the mud off, be quiet but definite about it. Do not poke the headcollar at him and expect him to put his nose in it; if he is the obliging kind he might do it, but he is more likely to move his head away from the irritation. Similarly, do not dab at his head with a brush; keep the strokes gentle but definite.

Nothing is more irritating than a pony that will not lead properly, and most parents find themselves having to lead at some time or another. So learn how to do it properly from the start – in theory you should stand at the pony's left shoulder, with your right hand holding the lead rope near his chin and the loose end in your left hand. Never wrap the rope round your hand, because if he shies or pulls away you could end up with broken fingers. If possible, always wear gloves for protection. It is also a good idea to tie a knot in the very end of the lead rope to prevent it being pulled right through the hand. As you step forwards the pony should step forwards with you, walking briskly but without pulling.

When turning, push the pony away from you so that you are on the outside of the bend. It is easier for him to stay balanced this way and you stand less risk of getting your toes trodden on. As an extra precaution, make sure you have sensible shoes or boots on. Trainers or high heels are lethal.

That is the theory. In practice, you might find that you have a dawdler who hangs back, or a puller who likes to charge off at the end of the rope. Both demand a quick cure.

With the reluctant pony, carry your daughter's whip and if the pony does not step forwards with you, say 'Walk on' in a firm but not loud tone and at the same time tap him in the girth area. It does not usually take long for him to connect the words with the tap. Make sure that you keep looking in the direction in which you want to go; never turn round to face the pony and pull him forwards. He will not like it, and will always be able to pull harder than you.

He will always be able to pull harder

Ponies who barge, either in the stable or when being led, must be persuaded of the error of their ways before someone gets trodden on or pushed over. Leading him in a bridle will give you more control, and if he tries to charge off, check him and put your elbow and shoulder into his chest. The reins should be brought over his head: keep the buckle end in your left hand and put your right hand on the reins near his chin, separating the reins with your index finger. Again use your voice, this time to say 'Wa-alk', drawing out the word. It is also advisable to use a bridle for extra control when leading on the road.

Teach him to move over in the stable by gently pushing where the rider's legs go and saying 'Over'; to get him to back-up, press against his chest and give the command 'Back'. If it does not work, get someone experienced to help you. A lot of it is confidence, and as you get to know the pony and he gets to know you the confidence will grow.

Moving home can make the calmest animal anxious, so do not be too alarmed if the quiet pony you tried and bought seems tense and worried for the first few days. He does not know where he is, he does not know the layout of his field or stable and he does not know you, so he is on the look out for potential dangers. Some ponies settle in a matter of hours, whereas with others it is a gradual process over a few weeks. All you can do is make the adjustment as easy as possible for him by establishing a new routine and sticking to it.

It is always a good idea to ask his previous owners to tell you about any of his 'funny little ways'. All ponies have their particular likes, dislikes and habits, just as people do. For instance, his old owners may have picked his feet out in the same order each time, starting with the left front hoof and hind hooves and then moving to the right hind and front ones. If you start with the right front hoof and then do the left one, he will no doubt pick his foot up when you ask him, but he might be a bit confused. Many ponies get so used to simple jobs like this being done in the same way that they pick their feet up in the right order without you asking them.

Ask the people you have bought the pony from if they can deliver him to his new home. No matter how many books you have read, you are bound to be slightly nervous about his arrival and whether you are going to cope, and your daughter will be excited, too. His old owners will at least know what his reactions mean and will be able to reassure him if he gets worried.

If he is going to live out all or most of the time he can usually go straight into his new field, provided you have checked the fencing and water supplies first. Hopefully he will not have to live by himself, so try to arrange his arrival when his companions are already turned out. The theoretical way of turning a pony out in his new field is to put him with just one quiet animal, but this is not always possible; he usually has to go straight out with all his future companions. The next stage can be a worry, because when a new pony is introduced to a group there is always a bit of squealing and kicking as the established ponies inspect the new arrival and they start to sort out the pecking order. One or more of them is likely to come in with kick or bite marks over the first few days, but there is no way of preventing it and it is very rare that the damage is any worse than superficial scrapes and nicks. Gently hose away any dirt, and puff with wound powder – read the first aid chapter next if you are the worrying kind!

Some books will tell you that you should lead the pony round his new field as soon as he arrives so that he knows where the fence and the water are, but while it is a good idea if you can do it, you might well find yourself in the middle of a group of curious ponies all trying to persuade the newcomer to show them what he is made of. It is a good idea to leave a headcollar on for the first few days to make catching him easier, but make sure it is a cheap chrome leather one that will break, not an unbreakable nylon one. Nylon headcollars

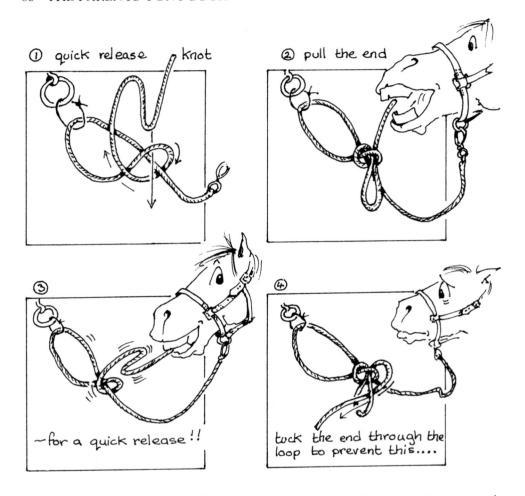

① quick release knot

② pull the end

③

~for a quick release !!

④

tuck the end through the loop to prevent this....

are fine for situations when the pony is under supervision, but it is not worth the risk of leaving him unattended in one.

Always use a quick-release knot to tie the pony up, and if he learns how to untie himself with his teeth (a favourite trick with many ponies) tuck the end of the rope through the loop of the knot. Always tie the rope to a loop of string or baling twine which is attached to the metal wall ring; this ensures that, should the pony pull back in panic, the string will break, and the pony will not damage himself.

Your daughter will be anxious to start riding her new pony and to show him off to her friends, but you must be firm and insist that they both have time to recover from the excitement of the move first. Let the pony spend his first day out in the field getting to know his surroundings and companions, and leave the first ride until the next day.

The first ride is the start of a 'getting to know each other' process. Although the pony will be obedient, he is probably used to being ridden by only one child, and although the basic aids or signals used by a rider are standard ones, everyone applies them in a slightly different way. Riding a new pony is a bit like learning a new language – even when you know the basics, it takes a while to become fluent.

If the ground is in good condition and there is an area in which your daughter can ride without the other ponies causing problems, encourage her to spend a few minutes practising starting, stopping and changing direction. It will probably do your nerves good, too, to see that she can walk and trot where and when she wants to. If they seem happy, let them enjoy their first ride out; keep it short and sensible, forty-five minutes to an hour on quiet roads.

Perhaps she has a sensible friend with a quiet pony who will go out with her. A new pony might be 'spooky' in new surroundings and prone to shying at things, but a quiet companion will give him confidence. If there is no one available to accompany her, ask your daughter if you can walk with her – she might be glad of some moral support! Walk at the pony's head, between him and the traffic, and do not hesitate to use hand signals to slow down approaching traffic. Most drivers are considerate, but a few do not realise that ponies can, and do, shy. It goes without saying that you should always thank considerate drivers and insist that your daughter does the same. A smile and an acknowledgement means that a driver might slow down for the next horse and rider, even if you had to ask him to do it this time.

Many otherwise knowledgeable people will describe some ponies as 'bomb-proof' which is rubbish; ponies shy and spook at things either because they are unsure of them or because they are feeling fresh and lively and a bit silly. The quietest pony can be startled by a sudden movement or noise, like a bird flying out of the hedge under his nose or a plastic bag blowing about. They are such creatures of habit that they will also shy at unfamiliar things in familiar places – for instance, your pony might not mind umbrellas, but if you stuck one in his field he would probably treat it with as much caution as if it were a wild animal. Keep talking to him and insist that he goes past the 'bogey', because obedience must always come first.

Boost your daughter's confidence and give yourself some peace of mind by booking some lessons for her with a good instructor. Hopefully the one who has taught her so far will be able to continue teaching her on her own pony, especially if you are keeping him at livery at the riding school, but if not she should be able to recommend someone who will teach her at home. Riding on your own is very different from riding in a controlled environment on riding school ponies who know the job better than their riders, and a weekly or fortnightly lesson will not only help them progress better as a partnership but will also iron out problems as soon as they arise.

No one wants to be a killjoy or a professional worrier, but it is sensible to lay down a few rules, and insist that everyone, including the pony, sticks to them. Always ensure that the pony is handled, and jobs are done, in the most correct and safe manner, thus establishing a good basis for a happy and enjoyable relationship with your pony. Never allow complacency to set in when handling ponies.

7 Feeding the Pony

Ponies, like people, need the right kind and the right amount of food to keep them fit and healthy. Their stomachs are very small and they cannot take in large amounts of food at one time; in the wild, nature takes care of this by ensuring that they spend most of their time grazing on pasture that is hopefully adequate but never too lush. A pony who lives out all or most of the time will in the main live as nature intended him to, but several important factors have to be taken into consideration.

For example, a wild horse needs only to survive and can do this by moving with the herd. Your pony does not need to worry about survival, but because he is working and, hopefully, living off better pasture than wild horses, his diet needs to be adjusted. If he is stabled part of the time, life becomes more complicated still.

Feeding is an art and a science – and it can also be a worry. Pick up any horse magazine and you will probably find features about feed supplements, allergies, probiotics and all sorts of complicated subjects. The good news is that as far as your pony is concerned you can ignore most of it, because by following a few golden rules you should be able to keep him happy and healthy.

Ponies, particularly the smaller native breeds, are notoriously 'good doers' and you will find that for some of the year grazing and a constant supply of clean water will be sufficient. In fact there are times when you will need to restrict your pony's grazing, because if it becomes too lush and rich and he gorges himself he could get laminitis, a painful disease colloquially known as 'fever in the feet'.

In late autumn and winter, when grass is scarce and what there is does not have a lot of goodness, you will need to supplement your pony's diet with hay and perhaps hard feed – usually in the form of specially prepared mixes or pony nuts. When you buy your pony, ask his previous owners to tell you what sort of work he has been doing and what he has had to eat, and this will give you a basis to work on. If you are keeping him at a livery yard or riding school, the owners will be able to advise you, but it is still important to understand the basics of feeding.

Just as someone doing hard physical work needs more calories than someone in a sedentary job, so a pony who is being ridden for an hour a day has different dietary requirements from a racehorse. It is as cruel to overfeed a pony as to underfeed him, because apart from increasing his susceptibility to laminitis it will put a strain on vital organs.

You should find that the pony kept on reasonable grazing will not need any other feed between about May to September, depending on the weather and his workload. If it is cold and rainy and you are expecting him to work hard, he might need extra. As with all feeding matters, if in doubt, ask your vet or instructor: never just hope for the best.

In the autumn and winter months he will also need hay, and if he is being worked hard he might need a daily hard feed. Before feeding concentrates, check with someone knowledgeable, preferably your instructor who knows both your daughter and the pony and can advise accordingly. Feedstuffs suitable for large ponies and horses can have a Jekyll and Hyde effect on small ponies: oats, for instance, can make them very 'hot' and silly and should never be fed.

Hay should always be of good quality. If it is dusty or mouldy, do not buy it; good hay smells clean and sweet and is springy to touch. It should always be at least six months old, because new hay can upset the pony's digestive system.

If the pony is kept at livery, you will probably be able to buy your hay from the yard owner as and when you need it. If not, you will have to buy your supply from a farmer or a feed merchant. How much you buy depends on your storage facilities, and obviously a large load will cost less per bale than a small one. Buying hay 'off the field' as soon as it is baled, and storing it until it is ready to feed, is the cheapest way, but if you do not have storage facilities you will have to buy it as and when you need it from your supplier.

Tell the supplier that the hay is for a pony; it must be of good quality, but you do not want the rich seed and clover hays that are fed to racehorses. The sort you *do* want is meadow hay or mixture hay, though meadow hay if becoming harder to find. When you get it home, store it on pallets and invest in a tarpaulin to keep the rain off.

Bad hay is worse than useless. Either your pony will not eat it, or the dust in it will make him cough. Long wet summers mean less hay can be produced, and what there is is not as good as it should be. In these circumstances, you are better off feeding good clean oat straw, but consult your vet if you are worried.

Occasionally ponies develop hay allergies, either because of dust, or chemicals that have been sprayed on the fields. All hay contains a tiny amount of dust, and in some cases you can solve the problem by putting it in a hay net and soaking it before you feed it. Another way is to put it into a large plastic bag like a dustbin liner (though not the sort that are impregnated with deodoriser to mask household smells) and pour three kettlesful of boiling water over it; tie the top of the bag and leave it for half an hour, and the steam will get to work to lay the dust.

If this does not work, you will have to feed some kind of hayage, made by harvesting the grass while it is still green and letting it dry in sealed containers. Richer than ordinary hay, it must be fed in smaller quantities.

The quantity of hay fed depends on the weather, the grass available and the pony's size and workload. As a very rough guide, reckon on about eight to twelve pounds a day for a 12.2 hh–13.2 hh pony. In bad weather, especially when the ground is frozen or covered in snow, he should have as much as he wants.

Ponies thrive on routine, so, as far as possible, feed at the same times each day. One feed a day is usually adequate for a pony living out, but in really bad weather he should be offered hay twice daily. If it is freezing, make sure you break the ice on his water supply, throw it out and top up with clean water.

Hay is usually fed in a haynet or on the ground. Both methods have their advantages and disadvantages – a haynet tied to the fence saves waste, but it must be tied high enough so that the pony cannot get his foot caught in it when it is empty. Tie a haynet so it will not come down as the pony pulls the hay through the mesh and remember that an empty or half empty net hangs lower than a full one. Feeding hay on the ground is quicker and safer, but more wasteful. Some inevitably gets trampled into the ground, and as ponies do not like dirty food it will not be eaten.

If more than one pony is being fed, it is worth putting out an extra pile or net. Ponies often squabble over food, and a spare portion means there is no danger of one pony being driven off hungry while an aggressive companion hogs two helpings.

A pony who is working hard, or who is stabled part of the time so that he can be made fit, will need hard feed, or concentrates, as well as hay. This will not usually apply to small ponies under 13 hh, so if yours belongs in this category ask your expert before putting him on a concentrate diet.

Concentrates are energy feeds, so quantities and types need to be carefully

tying a haynet

① pull the tie-rope through the ring

make sure this knot is not going to be in the way of your knot!

② put the end through the net as near the bottom as possible

③ pull up as high as you can and tie this release knot

~ poke the end back through the loop

④ this way the pony cannot undo the net, and.... it will not dangle dangerously low when it is empty!!

worked out. By far the easiest and most sensible way to feed them is to buy a reputable brand of coarse mix or horse and pony nuts, because these will already be nutritionally balanced by the manufacturers. Your feed merchant or supplier should be able to advise you on quantities, and most manufacturers have nutritionists who will give free advice by telephone.

Be realistic about your pony's workload. If he is only doing light work, do not feed him a high protein mix designed for the 'performance horse'! Nor should you feed vitamin and mineral supplements; these are for expert owners and animals in hard work. If you want to give him a treat, add some sliced apples or carrots to his feed; carrots should be sliced lengthways, to prevent the possibility of him choking on them.

Feeding is a fascinating subject, and you will find everyone has their own ideas on it. Experienced horse owners often like to feed rolled or bruised oats or barley and adjust the quantities themselves, but with a first pony it really is worth playing safe with a ready formulated feed. You need not worry that he is missing anything; the quantities of energy-giving ingredients have already been worked out. Provided you follow the manufacturer's instructions and feed the correct amount, your pony will not get silly on this feed, whereas feeding oats alone could give you more energy than you bargained for.

Types of feed: 1) a coarse mix, 2) pony nuts; both complete feeds. Pony nuts must not be confused with 3) sugar beet cubes, which must be soaked according to the manufacturers' instructions before feeding

When you buy hard feed, check the label on the bag to make sure that it is not out of date. Do not be tempted to stock up with too much in one go, or it will lose goodness before you get round to using it. The best way is usually to buy a month's supply at a time.

Always keep your feed in clean, dry containers with tight-fitting lids so that rats and mice cannot get into it. Purpose-made corn bins are nice but expensive – plastic dustbins are a perfectly adequate alternative for the pony owner.

Obviously the time you feed your pony has to fit in with things like school and work, but stick to a routine. It is not fair to feed him at nine o'clock in the morning one day and two in the afternoon the next. If feeding twice a day, split the total quantity into two equal portions and feed one in the morning and the other in the evening.

Life can get a bit complicated if a group of owners are sharing the same field. The best way is to try and arrange it so that all the ponies are fed at the same time, but if this is impossible and they have to be fed individually, do it out of sight of the others. It is no fun chasing off a group of jealous ponies while yours has his supper – and it is not fair on any of them.

Feed bowls and containers should be kept scrupulously clean; make it a rule to scrub out containers every time they are used. Some ponies love standing in them or tipping them over, so if yours is one of the destructive kind either buy a manger that hooks over the fence or door or stand his bucket in an old tyre.

If riding and feeding has to be combined in one visit, always delay exercise for at least an hour after feeding or you risk upsetting the pony's digestive system, perhaps giving him colic. Sometimes it is easier for your daughter to feed him after she has ridden, in which case it is important that he has cooled off and relaxed before being fed.

If you are interested in feeding, there are plenty of good books to tell you more about it. Many feed manufacturers also produce free leaflets that you can get from them direct or from your supplier, but, although full of good sense and well worth reading, they are inevitably produced as a marketing aid for their particular product.

It may be that the more you find out, the more confused you get. The answer is to keep calm and rely on some simple rules and the advice of someone you trust. There is an old saying that 'The eye of the master maketh the horse fat', in other words, get to know your own pony and watch out for changes in his behaviour or condition. If he is bright-eyed, with a healthy coat and is interested in life without being silly, there is not a lot wrong. If he is listless or his coat is dull and staring, or he has too much energy, something is wrong and you should ask for help.

A pony who is being fed properly should be well-covered without being fat. You should not be able to see his ribs, but nor should he resemble a barrel on four legs! Use the ten golden rules of feeding as your guidelines and you will not go far wrong:

1. Feed little and often. If your pony is living out he will take care of this himself, but if you are feeding concentrates remember that it is better to divide the amount into two small feeds rather than give him one big one.
2. Always feed the best quality hay and feed available. Poor quality stuff is false economy, because usually the pony will not eat it – and if he does, it will not do him any good.
3. Make sure that clean, fresh water is available all the time. A pony will often go thirsty rather than drink dirty water, so keep buckets and troughs well scrubbed. In winter, break and remove the ice at least twice a day and top up with clean water.
4. Make a routine and stick to it. Feed at the same time each day; it might be worth working out a rota with other pony families so that there is always someone to cover in an emergency.
5. If you have to change feedstuffs, do it gradually by mixing in a little of the new with the old and changing the proportions over a week or two. Sudden changes can play havoc with a pony's digestive system.
6. Different batches of feed can vary in weight, so invest in a spring balance (for your haynet) and a set of scales for hard feeds. It might sound fussy, but your pony will benefit and you will probably save money.
7. Always leave an hour between feeding and exercise, or the pony could get colic.
8. Keep feed containers and bowls scrupulously clean. Dirty ones attract rats and disease.
9. Work out feed quantities according to your pony's size, condition, temperament and workload.
10. Remember that native ponies are 'good doers' and it is as cruel to overfeed as to underfeed. If in doubt, always get expert advice.

8 The Stabled Pony

Looking after a pony who is stabled for part of the time means more work, but the same feeding guidelines apply. If he has to be stabled for a while because of illness or lameness, be sure to ask your vet about feeding. The sick pony will need hay to keep him occupied and to make up for not being able to graze, but concentrates will need to be cut right back and probably eliminated altogether to avoid causing more problems.

A stabled pony must have clean, fresh water available at all times and must be provided with a comfortable bed. This is to keep him warm and to give him the chance to lie down when he wants to; sometimes ponies will lie down in their fields, but there is a big difference between lying on grass and lying on concrete. If he tried to do the latter, which is unlikely, he would most likely scrape his legs or bang his hocks; ponies can also do this when their beds are too thin, so be generous. With capped hocks, the result of a bang on one or both hocks, fluid collects on the points, and they are a permanent and unsightly blemish. Some people will tell you that ponies can sleep standing up and do not need to lie down, but while they happily doze 'on the hoof' many like to lie down and stretch out.

Mucking Out and Bedding Down

For the maintenance of the pony's health and comfort he must be mucked out every day, even if he is only stabled at night. You also have to decide what sort of bedding to use and how you are going to get rid of manure. The most common bedding materials are straw and wood shavings, and what you choose really depends on availability and perhaps the personal preference of your yard owner. Some livery yards give you a choice, whereas others will only use one or the other.

Many like to lie down and stretch out

Straw is cheap and usually readily available, but if you are keeping the pony at home, you have to make sure you can get rid of the manure. Gardeners obviously like well-rotted horse manure, but big contractors will usually only take away heaps from larger yards. You might find that to get rid of the manure produced by one pony you have to bag it up in plastic sacks; some people manage to sell it, but others are happy to give it away. It all depends on where you live.

Shavings manure is not as popular with gardeners and nurseries as that produced from straw, and some do not like it at all. If you cannot get rid of it, it is best to burn it.

Livery yards and riding schools have their own arrangements for getting rid of manure, which makes life a lot easier. If you ever have your own yard, you will have to find a suitable site for the muck heap, remembering that if it is not downwind of houses and stables you are going to be very unpopular. Muck heaps attract flies; the muck heap site should, therefore, be as far from the stables as possible – without making trips to the heap an inconvenience – to prevent the stables and ponies being plagued by flies.

Wheat straw is the best and most common kind available, although you might be offered oat or barley straw. Try to avoid them because they are not as hard-wearing as wheat straw, flattening more quickly and giving the pony a thin, uncomfortable bed. Some ponies will eat their straw bedding; a little may not harm them, but too much is likely to cause colic, so if you arrive in the morning to find half the bed gone, try mixing up a dilute solution of disinfectant in one of the large plant sprayers and spraying it over the straw to discourage night-time nibbling.

Shavings are best bought from specialist suppliers and are often stocked by feed merchants and saddlers. You might also see timber yards advertising shavings for sale, and sometimes attractive prices are offered if you bag them up yourselves. The problem with timber yards is that it is too easy for nails and other foreign bodies to be swept up with the shavings, so do not risk it.

Shavings bales are bigger and much heavier than straw bales, and only older children will be able to manoeuvre them alone. Their advantage is that because they are wrapped in plastic they are easy to store, and you do not get bits blowing about all over the place.

Although straw and wood shavings are the most common bedding materials, you might come across shredded paper and peat. Shredded paper is dust-free, and for that reason sometimes used for horses and ponies with allergies, but the soiled bedding is hard to get rid of. It also seems to blow into every nook and cranny!

Peat is impractical, comes from environmentally sensitive sites, and should only be used as a last resort. It is very absorbent, becomes heavy to handle and will not keep your pony warm.

When you stable your pony for the first time make sure he has a nice deep bed, whatever material you are using. There should be no thin or bare patches and the bedding should be banked round the sides of the stable. This helps to lessen the risk of him getting cast, that is lying down in a position where he cannot move his legs properly to get up again.

Nothing looks nicer than a deep, clean bed. Enjoy the sight of it while you can, because it will look totally different in the morning! Then whoever is taking on the job of mucking out will have to get to work; some parents are happy to help out in the week, and it will certainly help keep you fit.

Like most jobs, mucking out is a lot easier if you have the right tools. The essentials for sorting out a straw bed are a four-pronged fork, a shovel, a stiff broom and a wheelbarrow. A full wheelbarrow can be heavy and difficult to steer, especially if your muck heap is some distance away, and one with two wheels is easier to handle than the usual one-wheeled garden wheelbarrow.

You will find that the more practice you have in mucking out, the quicker you will get. With straw beds, the easiest way is to do a complete job every day, but most people find shavings easiest to manage on what is called semi-deep litter.

With a straw bed, start by removing the visible piles of droppings. Some ponies are very clever at burying them, so sift through the straw with your fork. Then pick the cleanest corner of the box – some ponies always use the same spots as their toilet and leave others clean – and start sorting the straw into three lots, clean, slightly dirty and really dirty. The latter goes into your wheelbarrow and then on to the muck heap, and you will then be left with most of the floor and two corners of the box empty.

Using the brush and shovel, sweep the floor and collect the resulting dirty bedding to go on the wheelbarrow. Then shift your clean and slightly soiled piles of bedding into the newly swept corners, and sweep out the other two.

If the stable is going to be empty for a while it is a good idea to leave the bedding piled up so that the floor can dry. There are special products you can buy to get rid of smells, and scrubbing the floor with dilute disinfectant once a week helps keep the stable atmosphere healthy.

When putting down the bedding again, start by forking the slightly soiled pile – which will have dried out quite a bit by now – into the centre of the floor and bank the clean straw round the edges. Top up with fresh straw in the centre and if necessary round the sides and you have a nice comfortable bed for your pony.

A new shavings bed should meet the same criteria as a straw one and be deep, comfortable and banked well round the sides. Shavings settle as the pony moves around on them, so do not skimp on the first bed.

The easiest way of managing shavings is to remove the droppings and really wet patches every day without disturbing the whole lot. Use a rake or fork to level off the bed and top it up with clean shavings from the banks, finally building up the sides again with fresh ones. Once a week or once a fortnight, depending on how tidy or untidy your pony is in depositing his piles, muck out as for a straw bed, getting rid of all the wet shavings.

You can remove some of the droppings from a shavings bed with a fork, but the easiest way of picking up the rest is to don rubber gloves and do it by hand., It is not as bad as it sounds! Some people like to fork droppings and shavings into a wire basket, which they then shake so that clean shavings fall out.

If you have never mucked out a stable before, do not be too repelled by the thought of it. Horse droppings do not smell foul like other animals' droppings, and anyone who has changed a nappy will find mucking out child's play.

When mucking out the stable with the pony still in it, tie him up; although he might stand untied perfectly happily, there might also be the occasion when he decides to wander off, or leap over the wheelbarrow you have left in the doorway and hurt himself. It is safer, wherever possible, to tie the pony outside the stable or to turn him out.

For the same safety reasons, the pony should be tied up when you groom him in the stable.

He may leap over the wheelbarrow

9 Grooming

Grooming is a vital part of your pony's daily care. Obviously it makes him look smarter, but more importantly, it contributes to his well-being by caring for his skin and coat, and by providing opportunities for you to handle him and check him over for possible injuries. Muddy coats can hide a multitude of sins, and cuts or rubs spotted early can be dealt with much more easily than those that go unnoticed at first. The majority of ponies thoroughly enjoy being groomed as well.

The grooming routine for a pony kept at grass for all or most of the time is very different from that of the stabled pony who is protected from the elements. The latter is groomed more thoroughly, and with, in particular, the body brush (a short-haired brush) which gets deeper into the coat and removes the natural grease. His mane and tail can be pulled (thinned and shaped by pulling out hairs) and some people trim what they consider to be excess hair such as nose whiskers and fetlock hair.

The grass-kept pony, however, uses the grease in his coat as a water-proofing agent to help keep him warm and dry in bad weather. Similarly, the hair on his fetlocks (commonly known as feather) helps keep his heels dry. No matter how smart show ponies may look, never be tempted to cut off the grass-kept pony's whiskers – they act as feelers while he is grazing and warn him of anything that might hurt him if he touches it. Hair inside the ears is also there for protection and should be left alone.

Your pony's mane and tail are his protection against flies, so while it is possible to tidy them up, you should not resort to drastic pulling. A pulled tail, where hairs are taken out at the top and sides of the dock, leaves him no protection against insects in that sensitive area.

The basic grooming kit needed for a grass-kept pony is easy and cheap to put together. The handiest way to keep the items together is by storing them in a plastic box with separate compartments and a handle; you will find them in saddlers or in toolbox sections of DIY shops. It is a good idea to mark everything with your name, so that your brushes do not get mixed up with someone else's, and to tie a brightly coloured piece of string or wool to your hoofpick so it is easier to spot if you drop it. Each pony should have his own grooming kit to lessen the risk of spreading skin infections – do not lend or borrow kit, no matter how well you know the other pony and his owner!

Your basic grooming kit should have the following items:

Hoofpick   The most important item; care of the feet is a priority.

Dandy brush   A brush with long, stiff bristles for removing dried mud. Dandy brushes with soft bristles are excellent for getting mud out of manes and tails. Many people will tell you that you should never, ever, use anything but a body brush on these to avoid splitting the hair, but when they are caked with mud that theory does not always work. A soft dandy brush is effective and will not damage the hair.

Body brush   A brush with short bristles used mainly on stabled ponies, but which is useful for the heads, manes and tails of grass-kept ones.

Curry comb   The two main kinds are made from metal or rubber/plastic and are used for cleaning the body brush. Metal ones should *never* be used on the pony, unlike the rubber or plastic kind which are very useful for getting off dried mud, and for removing a loose winter coat.

Scrubbing brush   This is an unorthodox piece of grooming equipment that is nevertheless useful for scrubbing hooves – and saves wearing out your much more expensive water brush.

Sponge and cotton wool   The sponge is for cleaning the dock area, and should be kept solely for that purpose, and the cotton wool is for cleaning the eyes and nostrils; a separate piece for each area. Using the cotton wool once and throwing it away is more hygenic than using sponges for the eyes and nostrils.

Fly repellant   Essential in spring and summer; use a proprietary brand or make up your own. The old grooms swear by one part vinegar to three parts water and it seems to be effective as long as you do not mind the smell!

Stable rubber   Cloth used to wipe over the coat; a clean old tea towel does just as well.

Sweat scraper   A half-moon tough plastic blade with a handle, used to remove excess water or sweat from the coat.

The above should see you kitted out for everyday use, but you might want to add some or all of the following later on:

Water brush   Used to damp down (or lay) the pony's mane and tail.

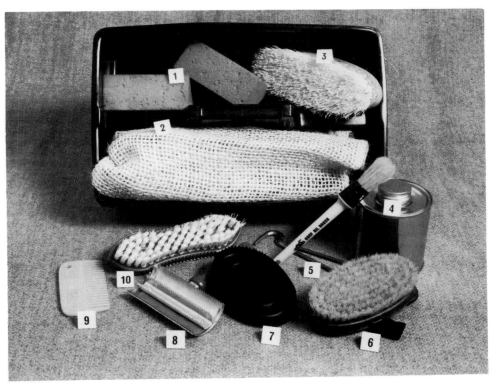

A grooming kit. 1) Sponges; 2) cactus cloth; 3) dandy brush; 4) hoof oil and brush for applying it; 5) hoofpick; 6) body brush; 7) rubber curry comb; 8) metal curry comb; 9) mane comb; 10) water brush

Mane comb   The plastic ones are less damaging than the metal kind but should still be used with care.

Pulling comb   Made from metal and has shorter teeth than the ordinary mane comb. Used for pulling the mane and tail.

Hoof oil/gel and brush   Most farriers say these preparations have more cosmetic than practical use; in really smart stables no horse is allowed out in public unless he has neatly oiled hooves. The solid kind is less messy to use . . . a tin of hoof oil goes a long, long way if spilled!

Cactus cloth   A rough fibre cloth that is excellent for removing grass and stable stains from grey ponies or those with white areas.

How to Groom

Tie up your pony and check him over. Run your hands down his legs to feel for any lumps, heat or cuts and then pick up his feet to check there is nothing obviously wrong.

Next examine the rest of him; is his coat in good condition for the time of year, or is it dull and staring? (Staring is when the hairs of the coat stand on end owing to bad health.) Are his eyes bright and clean, or are they sore and gummy at the corners – perhaps because of irritation from flies? As you run your hands over him, starting at the head and moving to the tail one side at a time, can you see or feel any injuries or rubs?

If all is well, start the grooming procedure by picking out his feet and checking the condition of his hooves and shoes as described in Chapter 10. Next use your dandy brush to remove any dried mud; brush in the direction of the hair in short movements. The 'textbook' grooming method says you should use the hand that is nearest to the pony's side, but there is nothing wrong with using the same hand all the time if you find it easier. If the dandy brush will not shift the dried mud, try the rubber or plastic curry comb in gentle circular movements.

Ponies have some particularly sensitive areas, so be very gentle when grooming them. The belly is often a ticklish place, and the head and lower legs (from the knee or hock down) are bony areas which makes them susceptible to knocks and bumps. *Never* use a curry comb on any of these areas; the soft body brush is the best tool. If there is a lot of mud on the head, rub it off with your hands, then use the body brush, not the dandy, to finish off. When the lower legs are particularly muddy, gentle use of the dandy brush will shift the worst of the mud, then, again, the body brush should be used.

When you have got all the mud off you will be left with a dusty pony. A long-haired dandy brush, used in short strokes with a flick of the hand at the end of each one, will disperse the dust so it, hopefully, will not settle back on his coat. A just-dampened stable rubber gets rid of any remaining dust.

Brush the pony's mane by throwing it over on to the 'wrong' side (i.e. the side where the mane does not lie naturally) and separating any tangles with your fingers. Brush with the body brush (or the soft dandy brush/plastic mane comb if caked with dried mud) then push back to the 'right' side and repeat.

To do his tail, stand to the side and put one hand on the dock to hold the tail out a little from the body. The hairs will fan out and you can deal with tangles or dried mud with the fingers before brushing out with the body brush or long-haired dandy brush. Some stables never allow any brushes to be used on their horses' tails, but insist that the grooms separate the hairs with their fingers to avoid splitting the hairs.

Clean the underneath of the dock with a sponge used only for that purpose, and wipe the eyes and nostrils with cotton wool.

If it is the 'fly season' your pony will benefit from the application of fly repellant, whether he is being ridden or turned out again. Beware of aerosol cans; the sound of these can launch some ponies into mid-air. If your pony is frightened, spray some repellant on to cotton wool and dab carefully round his eyes, flanks and girth area.

Even if he does not mind aerosols, remember that apart from damaging the ozone layer they are less economical than ordinary liquid kinds. You also need to cover gently one eye at a time with your hand when spraying his head to avoid repellant accidentally getting in and making them sore.

Dealing With a Wet Pony

There are bound to be occasions when the pony you catch is a wet, hairy monster covered with wet mud. He needs to be dried off before he can be ridden, and the easiest way to get rid of excess water on his neck and body is by using a plastic sweat scraper.

Then rub him down with a handful of hay or straw, or a couple of old towels, rubbing in the direction in which the coat lies. You should not saddle and ride a wet pony as this can set up a skin irritation; the quickest way to dry him off is by 'thatching'. This involves putting a layer of clean, dry hay or straw along his back and loins and fastening a sweat rug over the top. Put him in a stable or tie him up under cover and he should be dry enough to ride within an hour – do not leave him any longer, or he might start to sweat.

If he comes back wet from a ride, turn him out straight away so that he can have a roll and keep moving to dry himself off. If, however, your pony is turned out in a New Zealand rug, you cannot put it on him while he is wet, unless it is one of the latest ones incorporating high technology materials like Flectalon that allow you to do just that. Put such a rug on your shopping list and in the meantime thatch him as before, keep him warm and rug him up and turn him out as soon as he is dry.

Special Occasions

Most grass-kept ponies look hairy and scruffy in winter. When they get their summer coats they look totally different, and there are ways to make them

pulling a mane

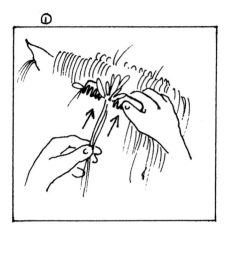

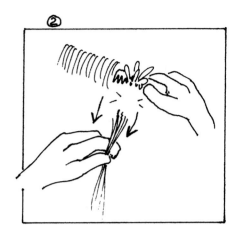

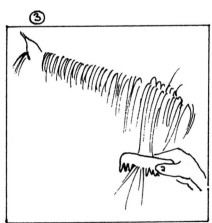

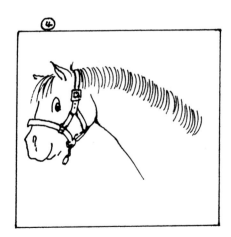

look even smarter for a show or other special occasion without removing their natural protection.

You should leave your pony's mane and tail as natural as possible, although his mane can be thinned and shortened a little by judicious use of a pulling comb. Only pull a few hairs at a time and always from underneath. Be kind and pull only when the pony is warm after exercise and the hairs come out easily, but be warned, it is too easy to get carried away.

Leave his tail full at the top by the dock, but cut level (banged) at the end. The correct length is about two inches below his hocks when he is moving. To achieve this correct length, ask someone to put an arm under his dock so that the tail is supported at the right angle. Run your hand down the tail, hold all the hairs together and try and cut in one movement.

Although grass-kept ponies should never have their whiskers or the inside of their ears trimmed, you can trim long hairs under the jawline. It is also acceptable to gently fold the edges of the ear together and trim hairs that stick out – but no more!

You may also take off a little, but not all, of the feather at his heels to neaten the appearance of his legs. Many of the pure-bred British native pony breeds are, however, expected to retain their feather in its natural state for the show ring. Check with the relevant breed society for guidelines on show turnout. (You will find addresses in publications such as the *Horse and Hound* diary, published every year.)

The easiest way to trim is to use a mane comb and blunt-ended scissors. Comb the hair up so it goes against its natural pattern and trim that which sticks out through the comb teeth. Feathering the scissor strokes gives an even better effect because it avoids obvious cut marks.

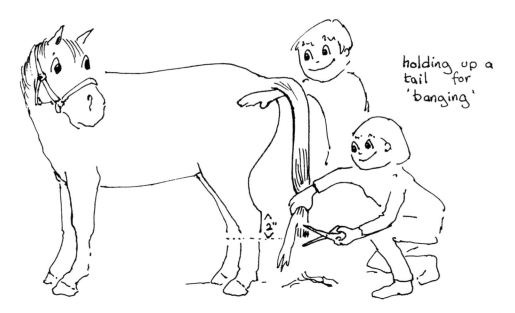

holding up a tail for 'banging'

PLAITING

Plaiting a pony's mane and sometimes his tail is done to enhance his appearance for shows and other events, though, again, pure-bred native ponies should be shown unplaited. It is one of those things which takes a lot of practice and is never quite as easy as books make it sound! Watching other people and then having a go by yourself on an amenable pony is the best way to perfect your technique.

_plaiting a mane

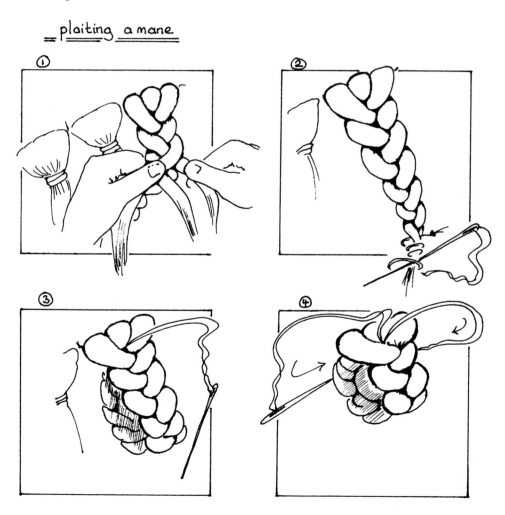

A mane that is to be plaited needs to be at least four inches and no longer than six inches long, and not too thick. These days it does not really matter how many plaits you do as long as there is an odd number down the neck and one for the forelock.

The mane should be clean and well-brushed, but do not wash it just before you plait or the hair will be too silky to stay in place. Damp it down, decide how many plaits you want and divide the mane into sections, fastening each one with a rubber band. For practice sessions you can fasten the finished plaits with rubber bands, but for shows they should be sewn. Use thick thread or darning wool the same colour as the mane, threaded through a large blunt needle.

Most people prefer to start near the ears and work down the neck, leaving the forelock until last, the reason being that a pony is more likely to toss his head when he gets bored, so you should get the plaiting in that area over with first. Working with a section at a time, make a firm, even plait as far down as you can.

When you get to the end, push your needle and thread (which should have a knot in it) through and round. If there are lots of straggly ends make another loop and pull tight right at the bottom to pull all the unplaitable ends together.

Double up the plait and push the needle through at the top, then roll the plait up and hold with a stitch to each side. Cut the thread close to the plait and fasten the needle securely to your clothing so you do not drop it and lose it. Once you have dropped a needle in a bed of shavings and had to empty the whole lot out because you cannot find it, you will never risk losing it again!

Perfect plaiting is an art in itself and experts can actually change the apparent shape of a horse's neck by the size and positioning of their plaits. In general a pony with a thick neck should have a larger number of thin plaits while a thinner neck is shown off best by the traditional seven plaits fastened on top of the neck to give the illusion of substance.

Some people like to use hair gel or spray to persuade wayward ends into place, but never cut them off, because when you take the plaits out you will be left with a row of bristles that looks awful and makes plaiting even harder the next time.

Do not leave plaits in for longer than a day and be careful when undoing them. Snip the thread with a pair of tiny scissors, avoiding the hair on each side; the pony will look as if he has had a perm when you unplait, but the waviness will soon disappear if you dampen the hair down.

A plaited tail can look really smart but again takes practice. Take a few hairs

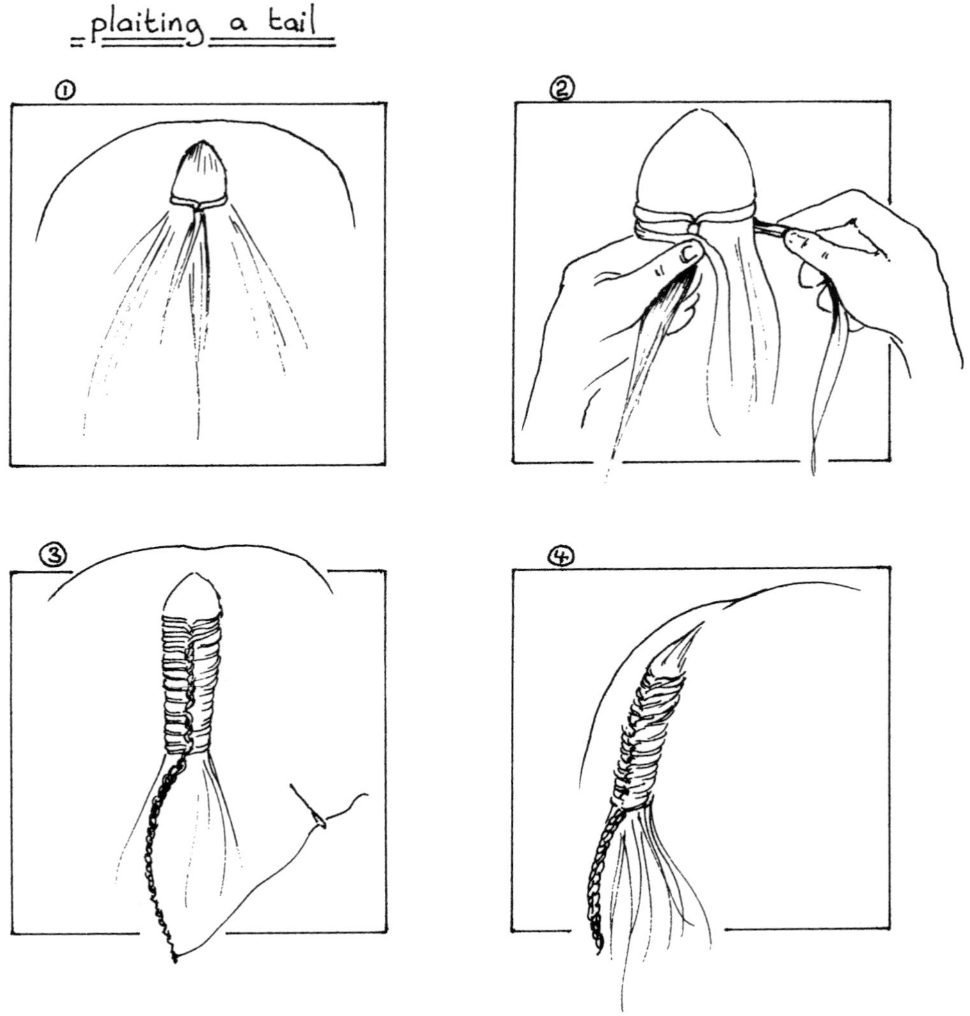

plaiting a tail

①

②

③

④

from each side, as high up the dock as you can, and sew them together to form a thin tail which will be the first centre section of your plait.

Now take thin sections – again, only a few hairs – from each side and plait. Take in another section every time you cross over from the sides until you are about two thirds of the way down the dock.

Carry on plaiting without taking in any more hairs from the side and when you get to the end fasten in the same way as your mane plaits. Double up to where you stopped taking in side sections, pass the needle through and make tiny stitches down the centre.

Expert tail plaiters say that the two most important things are to keep your middle plait in the centre and to pull the side sections tight as you take them across. Beware of taking too many hairs at a time.

10 Care of the Foot and Shoeing

The most important piece of equipment in your pony's grooming box is the hoofpick because correct care of his feet, both by your daughter and your farrier, is vital. There is an old saying, 'No foot, no horse', and like most old sayings, it contains an awful lot of truth.

If you tap the outside of your pony's hoof it will seem solid and unfeeling, but, although his feet stand up to a lot of hard wear, they are actually quite complex structures. The hooves bear his weight and act as shock absorbers so they must, therefore, be kept in the right shape, and if the pony is ridden on the roads he will also need shoeing regularly.

The outside of a hoof protects the sensitive parts inside, which include bones, nerves and blood vessels. A hoof is a bit like a fingernail in that it is continually growing; it starts from the coronet, the ridge at the top of the hoof, and grows down. When the pony stands normally you can see the outside, called the hoof wall, but if you pick his foot up you will see that the underneath is more complicated. The sole of the foot is reasonably tough, though it can be bruised if the pony treads on a sharp stone, but the V-shaped bit in the middle is much more sensitive and acts as a shock absorber. This V-shaped section is, for some reason, called the frog; my grandfather, who was a farrier for over sixty years, reckoned it was because it looked a bit like a frog's foot. Another, more colourful theory is that the old horse handlers would carry a special charm to help them handle restless horses. This was a frog or toad's bone that was the same shape as the frog in the hoof and was obtained in a peculiar ritual involving moonlight and a fast-flowing stream!

There are other, equally important parts to the foot that you cannot see, such as the laminae and the pedal and navicular bones – most good veterinary books have diagrams to show how well-designed a pony's legs and feet are.

A normal, healthy hoof grows about 2.5 cm a month. Horses in the wild

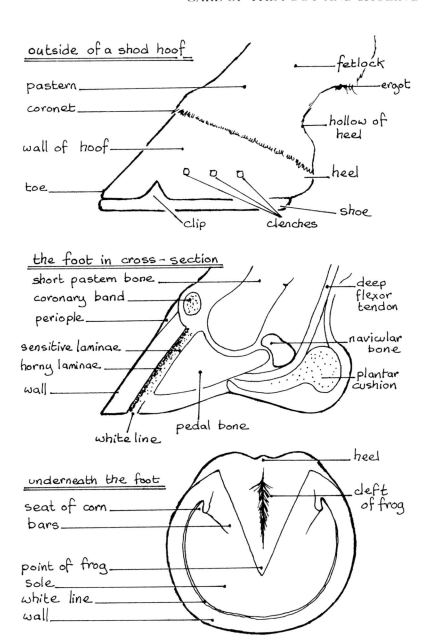

outside of a shod hoof

pastern
coronet
wall of hoof
toe
clip
clenches

fetlock
ergot
hollow of heel
heel
shoe

the foot in cross-section

short pastern bone
coronary band
periople
sensitive laminae
horny laminae
wall
white line
pedal bone

deep flexor tendon
navicular bone
plantar cushion

underneath the foot

seat of corn
bars
point of frog
sole
white line
wall

heel
cleft of frog

keep it worn down naturally, but if a pony was regularly exercised on the roads unshod the horn would be worn down too quickly and unevenly. For this reason, he must have his feet shaped and shoes put on by a good farrier. It is illegal for anyone who is not registered by the Farriers' Registration Council to shoe a horse, because bad trimming or shoeing can cause temporary or even permanent lameness.

It is illegal for anyone not registered by the Farriers' Registration Council to shoe a horse

The best way of finding a good farrier is by recommendation. If you keep your pony at livery you should find that they already have a good one who makes regular visits and all you need to do is make sure your pony is booked in and ready for him. If you are on your own, ask your instructor or other knowledgeable owners to recommend someone. If the people you bought the pony from are reasonably near, their farrier might carry on shoeing the pony for you. You might find that demand outstrips supply, so once you have found your farrier, make sure you are a good customer.

Helping the Farrier

When you catch the pony ready for the farrier's visit, ensure that his legs are clean, at least around the hooves and fetlock area, and the feet should be picked out. If conditions are muddy the farrier will not want to scrape off six inches of mud from the pony's legs and feet before he can start work. This is one of the few instances when it can be quickest and simplest to hose the mud off.

Not everyone has the luxury of a glamorous stable yard, but the farrier will not thank you for leaving him on his own to shoe a muddy pony in a muddy field. He needs to see what he is doing, and will not want to work in the pouring rain. Make sure that you have a dry, level, clean area that is free of wheelbarrows, forks or other obstacles. While the farrier is working it is best if the pony is not distracted – particularly if it is a youngster – by other ponies being fed or led past. If your pony has problems such as brushing or over-reaching, tell the farrier before he starts work. Brushing is when the inside of one hoof knocks the inside of its neighbour, thus causing cuts or bruising, as the pony moves. When a pony over-reaches it clips the heels of its forefeet with the toes of its hind feet.

Hold the pony unless you are sure he will behave when tied, and even if he is used to being tied when shod, it is sensible to stay with him, particularly if it is the first time the farrier has shod him. This also means you can watch the farrier at work. If he is busy he will not have time to stand and chat, but most are only too happy to explain what they are doing and advise you on how to look after your pony's feet between visits.

If the pony is to be shod in the stable, sweep the floor clean and make sure the stable is well lit.

Hot and Cold Shoeing

There are two forms of shoeing, hot and cold. The former method is the tradi-

Seeing a pony shod hot can be quite alarming the first time

tional one and generally thought to be the best, but cold shoeing by a good farrier is perfectly acceptable. These days most farriers who hot shoe have their own portable forges; in my grandfather's time, people would take their horses to his forge and he would make each shoe individually from iron bars. Nowadays ordinary shoes are usually made in factories from mild steel, and the farriers shape them as needed.

The advantage of hot shoeing is that if the shoe is not quite the right shape the farrier can alter it on the spot. If he knows your pony, he can usually do a good enough job at home to be able to shoe him cold, but, if possible, ask him to look at the pony's feet before shoeing him for the first time.

Seeing a pony being shod hot can seem quite alarming the first time, because there is lots of smoke and hissing sounds. But though you will smell burning when the farrier puts the hot shoe against the pony's foot, it will not hurt him. This part of the foot and the part where the nails go has no feeling; if a farrier makes a mistake and misjudges where the nail should go he can lame a pony, which shows how important it is to only use a registered farrier who has done the proper training.

Your pony will need a new set of shoes every four to six weeks, depending on how much he is ridden on the roads. But even if the shoes seem to have plenty of wear in them, he should never go longer than six weeks without seeing the farrier. His feet will at least need trimming and reshaping so that the shoes can be put back. When the same shoes are replaced they are called 'removes'. Some ponies wear out their hind shoes faster than their front ones, and this also needs to be taken into consideration.

Ask your farrier how often he thinks he should visit. Every time he comes, make your next booking and stick to it even if the pony's shoes look as if they will last a bit longer. A busy farrier will not appreciate a last minute cancellation, and you might find that he cannot fit you in again for a good few weeks. It also goes without saying that you should pay him promptly each time he comes, and the offer of a cup of tea or coffee is usually appreciated, if you have the facilities to make one! You will find that if you are a good customer, you will get good service from your farrier, and when you do get the inevitable emergency like a lost shoe, he will be much more likely to make special arrangements to fit you in.

Everyday Care of the Feet

The best farrier in the world cannot compensate for a lazy owner, so make sure that whoever takes care of the pony's day to day care realises how important it is to look after his feet. They should be picked out with a hoofpick at least once and preferably twice a day and it is a job your daughter should do both before and after she rides. Most ponies are pretty good at having their feet picked up, and some will obligingly lift them for you. Occasionally you will come across a pony who is awkward, so first of all try it by the book.

If you are picking up a foreleg, stand at his shoulder facing his tail and run your hand from his shoulder down his leg, avoiding any sudden movements. Close your hand round the fetlock and pull gently upwards. It helps to give a verbal command, like 'Up' or 'Foot up'; the pony will soon recognise this and should eventually react to the command alone. To pick up a hind leg, stand at his quarters, again facing his tail, and carry on as before.

That is the easy way, but occasionally you might get an awkward customer who refuses to pick his feet up, tries to lean on you or even kicks. If he will not pick his foot up, put your weight against his shoulder or quarters, and if you are dealing with a front foot try pushing his knee with your own or push your elbow behind his knee. Once he has picked his foot up, balance it lightly in your hand – if you do not give him anything to lean on, he cannot do it.

Ponies who kick are a menace and you should immediately get help from someone more experienced who can tell you if he is kicking because he is frightened, because something hurts or because he is bad mannered. Ponies usually kick backwards, so keep your arm on the inside of his leg so that you can let go without being hurt.

Use the hoofpick to clean out his feet and to check that his shoes are not loose. Starting at the heels and working towards the toe so that you are using a downwards movement, loosen and pick out any dirt and stones. Clean out all of the foot, being extra careful round the sensitive frog, taking care not to dig the hoofpick in there.

Keeping your pony's feet clean keeps them healthy. Dirty feet often lead to thrush. Regular picking out also means that there is less chance of a stone or even a nail being picked up and wedged into the pony's sole, causing soreness and possible lameness.

It is important to check your pony's shoes every day, and the easiest way of remembering is to make it part of the picking out routine. Start on the outside and see that the hoof is not growing over the shoe and that there are no splits in the horn (the horn is the substance, not unlike our fingernails, from which the hoof is constructed) or risen clenches. Clenches are the ends of the nails, which the farrier twists off and then knocks down. As the shoe wears thinner and the hoof grows, these rise up.

Next turn your attention to the shoe itself and slip the end of the hoofpick

The correct way to pick out a hoof. Use the hoof pick with downward strokes from heel to toe

between the shoe and the foot at the heel. If you can wiggle the shoe, it is coming loose. Listen to the sound a pony's shoes make on the road; a loose shoe will make a different noise from the others. Do not let your daughter ride the pony until the farrier has been and put things right, because a loose shoe can twist and pull off – it is too easy for the pony to trip and cut himself and perhaps be off work for much longer.

You may see ponies at shows with black, shiny hooves that have been painted with hoof oil. This is done purely for effect; most hoof oil is a waste of money, so do not buy any unless your vet or farrier recommends a special kind for a special purpose. Some oils have ingredients like lanolin that soak into the hoof and help to keep it in good condition, but make sure you're not allergic to it yourself. If it is recommended that you do use oil on your pony's hooves, do not apply it just before he is shod; the farrier does not want oil all over his hands.

Just as some people have weak fingernails, so some ponies seem to have weak, crumbling hooves. Dark horn is said to be stronger than white, but whatever colour your pony's feet are you can keep them as healthy as possible by feeding him properly and looking after them conscientiously. Your farrier might advise you to add a tablespoon of cod liver oil to his feed, or in really bad cases to consult your vet about a special supplement to strengthen horn growth. Remember, though, that any improvement is going to be slow and remedial measures taken in the winter might not show results until the following summer.

11 The Sick Pony

A well looked after pony will be happy and healthy, and prevention is definitely better than cure. However, it is inevitable that at some time your pony will become ill or will hurt himself. You will be able to treat most minor injuries and conditions yourself if you have someone knowledgeable to advise you, but if you are in any doubt you should call the vet. This does not mean that you should ring him about the slightest cough or cut, but it is better to be safe than sorry.

As part of your preventative policy, you should learn how your pony looks and behaves when he is in good health and be alert for any change. There are all sorts of warning signals to watch out for. If he suddenly becomes listless and apathetic, or goes off his food, he is feeling off-colour. Conversely, if he is restless and sweating it could be a sign that he is in pain, perhaps from colic.

Are his droppings of their usual consistency, or have they become either hard or runny? Is he struggling to stale (pass water)? Healthy urine is clear to pale yellow and there should be no sign of blood.

His winter coat will never be as sleek as his summer one, but it should not suddenly become dull and staring. Discharge from the nostrils, swollen glands under the jaw and a habitual cough are also danger signs. Look at the pony's eyes, too – they should be bright, and the lining membrane should be pink. If you are worried, ring your vet and explain the symptoms to him. He might ask you about the pony's breathing rate and temperature, so it is a good idea to learn to monitor these while your pony is healthy.

Breathing Rate

The normal breathing rate is eight to twelve breaths per minute while the pony is relaxed, and it should be even and regular. Stand behind him and you will be able to count as his ribcage rises and falls.

Temperature

Taking a pony's temperature is not as difficult as you might think and a normal reading is about 38°C (100.5°F), give or take half a degree. Any greater variation means you should consult your vet.

You can use an ordinary clinical thermometer, which has been shaken to get the mercury level down and greased with petroleum jelly, but a digital thermometer, which does not need shaking down and 'bleeps' when the temperature stabilises, makes life easier. The thermometer is inserted into the pony's rectum and held there for one minute to give you an accurate reading – do not let go of it, because if he contracts his muscles it could slip inside. Few ponies object to this process as long as you talk to them and run your hand over their quarters first so the contact does not come as a shock, but it is a good idea to get a helper to hold him rather than try and do it while he is tied up. Lift the tail slightly by putting your hand underneath the dock (the top of the tail) and put the thermometer in place with the other. When you have finished, wash the thermometer in tepid water containing disinfectant before using it again.

Back up your observation with regular worming, vaccination and teeth care programmes, all of which are vital and should never be skimped.

Worming

All horses and ponies have worms and you will never be able to eliminate them completely. The cycle starts when the grazing pony takes in larvae; they travel inside to the intestines and other organs, causing damage along the way, then develop into egg-laying worms passed out in droppings. A pony with a high worm burden will be thin with a pot belly. His coat will be dull and staring and he will be prone to colic.

You must control the parasite burden and break the worm cycle by regularly picking up droppings from the field and giving your pony doses of wormer every six to eight weeks. You should also make sure that the owners of ponies who share your field are equally conscientious.

When you have your pony vetted, ask the vet's advice about a suitable worming programme. There are lots of different brands, and worms can become immune to some of them if you use them all the time. Treatments come in paste, powder or granule form; the first comes in a kind of syringe and is

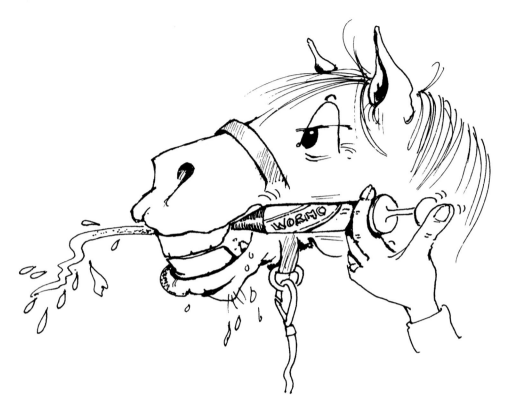

'Injecting' the wormer

'injected' on to the pony's tongue by gently inserting the syringe through the gap between his teeth, and the others are mixed with his feed. Paste is usually the best form as long as he is reasonably co-operative – some ponies can taste powders and granules even when well mixed in and will simply refuse to eat their food.

WORMS
There are four main types of worm that affect horses and ponies: white worms, seat worms, lung worms and red worms, and the degree of severity of damage and discomfort to the animal will vary.

The white worms may cause little problem to an adult equine, unless it is a large infestation when it can cause blockages of the gut, but could prove fatal in a young animal.

The seat worm lives in the rectum and causes an irritation around the anus and tail thus making the horse or pony rub his tail.

Lung worms live in the breathing tubes of the lungs, and horses and ponies with these worms will usually develop a cough. A cough is, however, also a symptom of other ailments and does not *automatically* mean the animal has lung worms.

An infestation of red worms is the most serious worm problem, and, again, in the young animal can cause death. These worms migrate through the system via the gut wall and into the internal organs and blood vessels.

Vaccination

You will need to have your pony vaccinated against tetanus and equine influenza. Hopefully his previous owners will have kept his protection up-to-date and you will simply have to arrange for yearly boosters. If he has never been vaccinated or is over the time limit, you will have to start from scratch with a new course, which your vet will advise you on.

Some people might tell you not to have your pony vaccinated against equine 'flu in case he has an adverse reaction to it. However, most vets say that reaction is minimal, and equine 'flu is both highly infectious and can permanently damage your pony's health.

Tetanus is a killer – of people, as well as horses. So do make sure that not only your pony but also your daughter and anyone else in the family involved in outdoor activities is protected. Your GP will arrange for the human injections and once you have had the initial course you only need a booster once every ten years.

Teeth

When you pony has his annual vaccinations, ask the vet to check and, if necessary, rasp his teeth. If these wear unevenly they can get sharp edges which are not only painful but can stop the pony grinding his food and so digesting it properly.

Sharp teeth can also cause problems with the bit, because if a pony's mouth hurts he will understandably protest. Pulling and head-shaking can be caused by teeth in bad condition.

Observation

The big difference between a sick person and a sick pony is of course that the pony cannot tell you how he feels or which bit hurts – so it is vital to be observant. A friend who lets a family keep their pony at grass livery with her noticed that he looked a bit listless, and when she mentioned this to the little girl she confirmed that he was quieter than usual to ride. The pony's temperature proved to be higher than it should have been, so he was brought in to a spare stable and the vet sent for. It turned out that the pony had a liver infection that could have proved fatal; luckily it was noticed and treated in time, but it just goes to show how important it is to get to know your pony.

First Aid

You should also make up a first-aid box containing a few essential items. As time goes on you will probably add to it – but be as careful with medication for animals as you are for people. If a vet prescribes a course of drugs, do not stop halfway through because the pony seems back to his normal self. Keep an eye on 'use by' dates, and get rid of anything that is over the limit.

The following items make up a useful first-aid box that should always be on hand, whether you are at home or at a show or other event:

Animalintex poultice
Antibiotic wound powder in 'puffer' bottle
Bandages – crepe bandages are a must, and the kind that sticks to itself as it is applied round the leg makes a useful addition
Cotton wool and cotton wool buds
Gauze or lint dressings
Hydrogen peroxide
Scissors with rounded ends
Zinc and castor oil ointment

Bandages and Bandaging

To ensure the pony is warm and comfortable, your vet may advise you to rug him up and put stable bandages on; bandaging is not difficult, but is something that should be practised before you actually have to do it! Always remember that if you bandage one leg, you should also bandage the opposite leg. If a pony hurts one leg he will put more weight on the opposite one, so you have to give him extra support.

Stable bandages are about four inches wide and are put on over padding

putting on a stable bandage

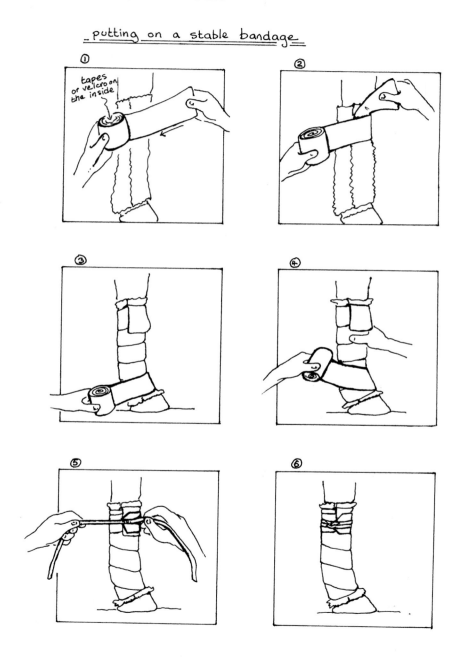

(usually gamgee, available from saddlers) to help lessen the danger of them being fastened too tight and damaging the tendons. Bandages on the front legs go from just below the knee to the coronet, and the hind ones start just below the hock and go to the coronet.

Before starting, check that any tapes or Velcro fastenings are rolled to the inside. Hold the bandage at a slight angle to the leg and leave a loose end about four inches long; make your first turn, then either fold the loose end down and wrap the bandage over it with the second turn, or bandage the loose end in on the return journey before fastening the bandage. This helps to keep the bandage secure. Each turn overlaps the previous one by a third to a half of the bandage's width, depending on the size of the pony's leg.

When you get down to the coronet, the band at the top of the hoof, you will find that the shape of the pony's leg makes it easy to turn and bandage back up the leg. Aim to finish where you started, making sure that tapes or fastenings are on the outside or inside of the leg. Never tie tapes so that the knot is on the front, where it will press on the bone, or the back, where it will be against the tendons.

To remove the stable bandages, undo the fastenings and unwrap, passing the bandage from hand to hand. Don't try and roll it up as you go, because if the pony fidgets he could get tangled up and frighten himself. Roll up with the tapes to the inside so the bandages are ready for use again.

Daily Care of the Invalid

A sick pony demands the same consideration you would give a sick person; warmth, comfort, peace, quiet and a modified diet. If your pony is confined to a stable for a while he will not be getting any exercise, so his diet must be adjusted. Unless your vet says otherwise, simply give him good quality hay and a constant supply of clean water.

Your vet may ask you to give him a bran mash, which has a laxative effect. Put a scoop of bran into a bucket and pour boiling water over it until all the flakes are wet. Add an ounce of salt, then cover and leave to cool. A sliced carrot or apple added to it might tempt a pony who has lost his appetite.

While you will need to keep an eye on your pony, do not fuss round him too much – think how you feel when you have 'flu! Do not groom him, simply pick his feet out daily and muck out round him, disturbing him as little as possible.

12 Common Ailments

Just as reading a medical dictionary turns most of us into hypochondriacs, so a section on some of the ills which can beset your pony can seem a bit frightening. The answer is not to panic about what could happen, simply to be aware of it and have an idea of what action to take.

Bot Flies

The bot fly is a summer visitor and, in appearance, resembles a bumble bee. It lays its eggs on the tips of the hairs of the pony's forelegs and forequarters; a region within reach of the pony's tongue, and from where they can be licked off. The larvæ then travel from the mouth to the stomach and attach themselves to the stomach wall. Having spent the winter feeding on the pony's food, they are ejected with the droppings in the spring and develop into adult flies. The cycle then starts again.

A heavy infestation can affect the pony's condition and cause colic, and must be treated by a vet.

To help prevent this problem, examine the pony closely, and when the eggs are present remove them with a special bot-removing knife available from saddlers.

Colic

Colic is painful, as anyone who has ever suffered with a stomach ache will know. In horses it can be fatal, so this is one time when you should call the vet at the first signs of an attack so that he can give the animal something to relieve the pain.

The commonest cause of colic is worm damage, which underlines the importance of an effective worming and paddock-care programme. It can also be brought on by allowing a pony to drink a large amount of cold water, or to eat food that ferments, like grass clippings. So if your field is overlooked by gardens, make sure the owners are not tipping their lawn mowings into it.

Early signs of colic include lethargy and a reluctance to move. The pony may sweat, look at his flanks or try to kick his belly. As the pain gets worse, he will often try and roll – but you must not let him. Rolling is the easiest way to cause a twisted gut (a twist in the intestine) and though surgery might be able to correct it, the operation does not always work and the pony has to be put down.

If you think your pony might have colic, ring the vet straight away, if possible taking the pony's temperature first. Depending on the severity of the symptoms, he will tell you what to do until he gets there.

Cracked Heels

Cracked heels is a painful condition in which the skin on the heels is affected by dermatitis. The skin becomes red and sore and then cracks; in bad cases the pony can go lame. Wash the affected areas with a medicated cleanser like Hibiscrub and then apply a soothing cream such as zinc and castor oil ointment. It is generally believed that both cracked heels and mud fever (see appropriate section) are aggravated by washing legs in cold weather to get the mud off, so where possible let the mud dry and then brush it off.

In bad weather this is easier said than done. Through trial and error I have found that I get the best results by hosing the mud off, then drying the legs and heels thoroughly with towels (you can even use a hairdryer with a quiet pony). When the pony is dry, apply the udder cream that is used for cows with mastitis as a barrier cream – you can get it from most agricultural merchants and a big tub lasts for ages.

Cuts and Wounds

Small cuts and grazes are easily dealt with, but should never be discounted. If left unattended they can get infected, so check your pony over once a day and make sure that there are no cuts or scratches under the mud, especially on his legs.

The first step is to clean the wound, using a saline solution (one teaspoon of salt to a pint of warm water). Soak a wad of cotton wool and hold it above the injury, gently trickling the water on to it.

If there is some swelling, perhaps because the pony has been kicked, cold hosing can help to reduce it. Start by turning the hose on very gently and trickling it on the ground near the pony, then run the water on to his hoof and gradually up his leg until the water is running down over the wound. Some ponies are suspicious, not of the water, but of the hose pipe (the theory is because they have an instinctive fear of snakes!) so let him have a good look at it if necessary. Once the wound is clean, puff on some wound powder.

Puncture wounds are often caused by the pony treading or pushing against something like a nail or thorn. Because they are so small they are easy to miss, and because they are deep-seated they can cause a lot of trouble. They need to be poulticed using Animalintex; prepare it according to the manufacturer's instructions on the packet, then cover it with something waterproof: clingfilm is ideal as it sticks to itself, but you can also use a cut-up plastic bag. Bandage over the top and leave until the poultice cools, and when you remove it you should see the infected matter that has been drawn out. Repeat the process until there is no more discharge.

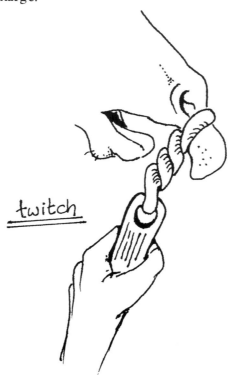

twitch

To poultice a hoof, cut an appropriately shaped piece of Animalintex and prepare as before. Then tie a plastic bag over the pony's hoof and the corner of a cut-down sack over that. Keep an eye on him to make sure that he does not split it, because it is important that no dirt gets to the wound.

In theory ponies stand perfectly still while you minister to them; some are amazingly co-operative, but others can react violently, which is hardly surprising, as it probably hurts. You will have more control over a pony in a bridle than in a headcollar, and if he tries to kick, hold up a foreleg. It can sometimes be kinder in the long run – and safer – to use a twitch, a loop of thin rope fastened to the end of a wooden handle and twisted round the pony's upper lip. This might sound cruel, but vets now say that it is perfectly painless and acts on an acupuncture point, releasing natural pain killers. Even so, a twitch should only be used by someone who has been taught its proper use; get your expert to show you.

More severe wounds that look as if they might need stitching obviously need a vet's attention. Clean them, but do not put anything on them – it complicates the vet's job if he has to take it off again before carrying out his own treatment.

If a wound is spurting bright red blood, it means the pony has severed an artery and you should put in an emergency call to your vet. Keep the pony still, put a gauze or lint dressing over the wound and bandage tightly over it; the pressure will slow down the bleeding until the vet arrives. Old textbooks will tell you to make a tourniquet, but modern opinion advises against this.

Galls

Saddle and girth galls are sores caused by badly fitting or stiff, badly cared for tack. They usually begin as swellings and treatment depends on whether the skin is broken or not. If it is unbroken, apply salt solution or witch hazel to toughen the skin; if it is broken, bathe with a pint of warm water containing a teaspoon of salt and puff on antibiotic powder. The pony must not be ridden until the galls have healed and you should get the fit and condition of your tack checked by an expert. Make sure, too, that the pony is tacked up correctly. The saddle must be slid back into place so that the hairs lie flat underneath it, the girth must be tightened gradually and the forelegs pulled forwards before mounting so there are no folds of skin pinched round it.

If the swellings are in the girth area and are followed by hair loss, leaving round patches, they are probably not girth galls but ringworm (see the ringworm section).

Hay Allergy

Hay allergy is one of the commonest respiratory problems and you should consult your vet if your pony coughs repeatedly or has laboured breathing. Usually the problem is dust, though sometimes the chemicals sprayed on fields are blamed. In mild cases, you can relieve the allergy by soaking or steaming hay. Soak the pony's haynet in clean water for half an hour before feeding or put it in a dustbin bag, pour on three kettlesful of boiling water and tie the top. Leave for half an hour before feeding.

More severe cases mean you will have to feed hayage, a dust-free product sold under names like Horsehage and Propack. Because it is higher in protein than ordinary hay you need to feed less; make it last longer for a greedy pony by feeding it in a special small-mesh haynet.

Ponies with hay allergy should be stabled on shavings rather than straw and you must ensure that there is adequate ventilation.

Lameness

When you watch a sound pony trot, his steps should be rhythmical and of the same length. If he seems uneven, he is probably lame. Severe lameness will show at the walk, but, with less severe lameness, it is more usual for the walk to appear normal; the trot is the gait that shows it up, so this is the gait we use to identify the source.

If the pony goes lame while your daughter is riding him or if he is obviously unsound when you lead him in from the field, look for the obvious causes first. Perhaps a stone is trapped in his foot, or maybe he has been kicked. If there are no obvious reasons for the lameness he must be led home; never ride a lame pony.

Put a headcollar or bridle on the pony and get someone to walk and then trot him up in hand on ground that is hard and as level as possible. The reins or headcollar rope should be kept loose, so that he has freedom to move his head and neck, and you should stand so that you can see him moving towards you, then in front of you and finally away from you.

The first thing you have to find out is whether he is lame in front or behind. If he is lame in one front leg his head will nod as the sound leg hits the ground and go up again as the lame and therefore painful leg takes his weight. It is rare for a pony to be lame in both forelegs, but if he is he will be reluctant to stride out and will probably hold his head higher than usual. Hind leg lameness is more difficult to spot, but if you watch the pony carefully you will see him put more weight on the sound leg. If you are not sure you can tell where the problem is, ask someone with more experience to watch as you trot the pony up.

The next step is to pinpoint the exact trouble spot. Run your hands down his leg and over the foot, comparing them with their opposite numbers; for instance, if the pony appears to be lame in the near fore, see how it feels compared with the off fore. Is there heat in any part of the lame leg or foot? Are there any swellings or lumps where there were none before?

If there are no signs of heat or swelling the most likely explanation is that the lameness is in the foot. Call your farrier and explain what is wrong; if he is not able to come out and have a look fairly soon, call the vet instead. The pony may have a bruised sole or a corn (bruises in the heel area) and he will be able to take the necessary action and tell you how to continue the care. Bruised soles usually need poulticing, and if your pony has naturally thin ones or his feet are flat the farrier might advise shoeing him with a leather insert between the shoe and the sole. Corns are usually cut out and the foot poulticed.

Another possible cause of lameness is a pricked foot, which means that a nail has been driven too close to the sensitive part of the foot. Only the blacksmith or vet will be able to spot this and the pony will usually go sound as soon as the offending nail is removed. If he does not, it means the nail hole has become infected and is therefore a puncture wound to be treated by poulticing.

Any heat or swelling in the tendon or ligament areas (between the knee or hock and fetlock) should get urgent attention from your vet. If these are sprained and you continue to ride the pony he could end up out of action for up to a year. Cold water hosing is the best immediate first aid, but be sure to follow your vet's instructions exactly.

Capped hocks, swellings on the points of the hocks where fluid has collected, are usually caused by the pony scraping his legs on a bare stable floor, so it is important to give him a deep bed. They can also be caused by him rolling on hard ground and scraping his hocks when he gets up, or by kicking against the wall of a trailer or horsebox. Alternate cold hosing and hot fomentation can help to get the swelling down in the first place, and your vet will be able to give you a special powder that is mixed up to a paste and applied to the hocks as soon as possible.

To foment, use water as hot as you can comfortably bear to put your hand in, and squares of towelling or blankets: old facecloths are ideal. Soak the material and hold it against the site until it starts to cool, repeating the process with more hot water.

Rest is usually the cure for lameness where there is no obvious cause, but if a pony is still unsound after two or three days or if the lameness recurs, call your vet. Recurrent lameness may indicate navicular disease (see navicular entry).

Laminitis

Laminitis, or 'fever in the feet' as it is commonly known, is a danger that all pony owners must beware of. It is usually caused by too much good grass and is a painful condition of the sensitive part of the pony's feet. There will be noticeable heat in his feet and he will be reluctant to move; when he does he will hobble rather than walk. When he stands, he will often push his front legs as far in front of him as he can to try and relieve the pain.

Prevention is better than cure, so restrict the pony's grazing when it is at its most lush. Your vet will be able to give him drugs to relieve the pain and help the condition, but in really bad cases the pony may have to be put down – early vigilance can prevent this.

Lice

If your pony's winter coat is dull and he seems to be itchy – especially in the head and neck areas – he could have lice. You can usually spot them moving about in the coat; they are whitish yellow and very small, about the size of a pinhead. They do not affect humans and are easily got rid of by dusting the pony with louse powder.

Mud Fever

Similar to cracked heels and treated in the same way. The area below the fetlock is usually affected and white legs are more prone to it than dark ones. Gently pick off the scabs or remove them with a cleanser like Hibiscrub, then apply zinc and castor oil ointment or udder cream.

Navicular Disease

A disease of the navicular bone in the foot. Warning signs include recurrent lameness, when the pony characteristically starts off lame and improves with work, coupled with resting a foreleg (though do not assume that because your pony rests a foreleg he has navicular disease!).

Your vet will be able to help with drug treatment, and special shoeing can help keep the pony sound. Navicular can be treated but cures are unlikely. It rarely affects animals under 14.2 hh.

Rain Scald

A similar infection to mud fever and cracked heels that develops on the back and hindquarters of horses at grass whose coats frequently get wet. Remove the matted hair and scabs and treat as for mud fever or cracked heels.

Ringworm

Ringworm is an infectious fungal disease that is spread through contact. Humans can get it, too, so if your pony contracts it be careful about hygiene.

It usually starts on the head and neck or saddle area, especially round the girth. Early signs are swellings where the hair stands away from the skin, followed by hair loss leaving bald, scaly patches that are usually round.

If you suspect your pony has it, get veterinary advice immediately. Check and keep an eye on other ponies he has been in contact with, and if they show signs they must obviously be treated as well. Your vet will give you powders which are mixed in water and applied to the affected areas and probably others which are mixed in with the pony's feed. Follow the instructions exactly and remember that you must disinfect everything the pony has been in contact with, using a disinfectant that will kill ringworm (not all of them do); that means tack, rugs, grooming kit and stable. Bedding should be burned and replaced with fresh.

Do not let your pony come into contact with others until the condition has cleared up. A sensible precaution is never to use someone else's grooming kit or girth, or let them use yours on another pony.

Strangles

Strangles is a highly infectious respiratory disease. Isolate the pony immediately strangles is suspected and call the vet. Signs of the disease are a thick nasal discharge and the formation of an abscess under the jaw. Antibiotics may be needed to treat the disease.

As with ringworm, disinfect everything the pony has been in contact with, and do not swap tack or grooming kit with other owners.

Sweet Itch

Sweet itch is a distressing condition which affects some ponies in summer and can make them rub their manes and tails bare. It is an allergy to a biting mosquito, and the best way of dealing with it is to stable the pony while the midges are at their most active in the early evening and treat him with fly repellant. You can also buy soothing lotions to ease the itching and stop the pony rubbing.

Thrush

If your pony has thrush in his feet, you will probably smell it. The outer layers of the frog become soft and there is a very unpleasant odour. Poor hygiene is a contributory factor to thrush. It will help to prevent the disease if the pony's feet are picked out at least once a day, and if the stable-kept pony is mucked out daily so that he is not standing in dirty bedding.

Ponies with upright, 'boxy' feet are particularly prone to it, and sometimes the best you can do is keep it at bay.

Your farrier will keep the frogs as healthy as he can by cutting away dead tissue, after which you can use antiobiotic sprays (usually purple so you can

Thrush

see exactly where the spray is going, so be careful not to get it on clothes) or hydrogen peroxide. It also helps to keep the feet as dry as possible, but that is easier said than done with a grass-kept pony in winter.

Warble Flies

These parasites are more common in cattle than horses, but can cause a great deal of pain and damage to a horse. Another summertime visitor, the warble fly lays its eggs on the pony's legs where they hatch into larvae. The larvae migrate to the pony's back, under the skin, and usually settle under the saddle area. They lie under the skin forming painful lumps, until, in due course, they should emerge through the skin to develop into flies. However, in horses, the larvae often die under the skin and have to be removed by the vet. The resulting sore takes a long time to heal and, if in the saddle area, should not have a saddle placed on them until completely healed.

13 Safety and Security

Environment

Stables and fields should be checked regularly. All broken wooden fencing and gates must be repaired immediately, and protruding nails removed, replaced or hammered in so that they are not a danger. Sagging wire fencing must be tightened to stop ponies trampling it down to get out, and if ponies paw at sagging wire they may get their legs through the fence or caught up in it. Gaps in hedges must be filled, and poisonous plants removed from the field. If your field is next to a road, you may find rubbish being thrown into it which must be cleared regularly.

Clothing

It is a favourite joke that horsey people always wear waxed jackets and green wellington boots with buckles on the side. They often do, because they are both comfortable and practical, but there are times when the right kind of clothing is vital.

As far as your daughter is concerned, it should be an unbreakable rule that she never gets on any pony without wearing a proper hat and safe footwear – even if she is only coming from the field to the yard. A proper hat is one that carries the BSI numbers 6473 or 4472: some meet both standards. If she takes part in any Pony Club activities she will have to comply with its rule specifying that headgear must carry the 4472 standard. From time to time improvements may be made and the BSI standard numbers may change. It is advisable to check these details before purchasing a hat.

Even the best hat is, of course, only any good if it is fitted and worn correctly. Never buy a secondhand hat, because you do not know if the previous wearer had a bad fall. Go to a reputable retailer – preferably one who

BSI standard headgear should always be worn when riding. Chimene, left, wears a hard hat which meets both 6473 and 4472 standards, and Amanda wears a 4472 skull cap; its cover is called a silk

has the British Equestrian Trade Association hat-fitting diploma. Finally, you must always ensure that the safety harness is fastened.

Sadly, you will probably notice that many leading riders in the show jumping, showing and dressage worlds wear hats without safety harnesses unless competition rules specify otherwise. Quite frankly, it is a shame they do not set a better example to the children who look up to them.

Safe footwear is another important consideration. Assuming that the stirrup irons are the correct size and the rider's foot can neither get trapped because they are too small nor slip all the way through because they are too big, then the next safety check is your daughter's footwear. Trainers or wellingtons with ridged soles are definitely not suitable, the former because they can allow the foot to slip through the iron and the latter because they can trap the foot in the iron. Proper riding boots are the safest option, especially jodhpur boots with blocked toes. These can save a lot of pain and blackened toenails if hoof treads on foot!

You need to pay attention to your own wardrobe, too. Shoes with high heels are useless; I know one mum who manages to look immaculate in skirts and wellingtons, but most go for jeans. Wellingtons are fine and practical in wet weather, and you will find that the ones with the buckles on the side are actually more comfortable than cheap ones. The rubber is stronger and more flexible, so they do not chafe if you wear them for long periods, and the buckles allow you to adjust the fit at the top. If you wonder why this adjustment is necessary, try walking through a boggy field in ordinary wellingtons without losing them in the mud. In summer, a pair of leather jodhpur boots is a good investment. Leather breathes, so your feet do not sweat, and the blocked toes will protect your toes if the pony stands on them. Treat the boots with dubbin and they will keep your feet dry, too.

As far as the rest of your wardrobe goes, it is a matter of personal taste. Natural fibres are more comfortable than synthetic ones and you need to be prepared for the fact that the British weather can and probably will do what you least expect. A waterproof jacket in waxed or oiled cotton or one of the new 'breathable' fabrics will give you real value for money, because you can wear it just about anywhere with anything. A lightweight duvet waistcoat gives warmth without bulk and on really awful days you can wear it under your waterproof jacket and stay warm and dry. Finally, remember that you lose most heat through your extremities; on cold days wool gloves and socks (not nylon ones) and a hat or headscarf will make life much more bearable.

Road Safety

Everyone has to ride on the roads these days, and a child on a pony is in some ways even more vulnerable than a child on a bicycle. A bicycle will not shy if a paper bag blows out in front of it, or take fright if a car goes past too fast and too close. Most motorists are considerate, but some overtake riders in ways that can only be described as dangerous. Usually this is through ignorance, but ignorance is no excuse in the case of an accident.

There are no complete records of horse-related accidents, because the traffic accident report used by police makes no specific reference to horses and simply includes them amongst 'carriageway hazards'. However, statistics from the

British Horse Society show that there are eight accidents involving horses every day.

Dr Helen Muir and her team at Cranfield Institute of Technology began analysing the BHS's accident report forms – voluntarily filled in by people unlucky enough to be involved in an accident – in 1985. Through her work it is possible to give a picture of the typical horse-related accident: it commonly occurs in daylight and at the weekend, between 10 am and 5 pm, in rural areas, on minor roads and in light traffic. These are probably the safest conditions most of us can find to ride in, so how do we help to cut down the accident figures?

You can help by ensuring that your daughter is aware of the dangers and knows how to ride on the roads in maximum safety. Buy a copy of the British Horse Society booklet *Riding and Roadcraft*, available from the BHS at the British Equestrian Centre, Stoneleigh, Kenilworth, Warwickshire CV8 2LR, and go through it together from cover to cover. Ask at your local riding school about arrangements for taking the BHS riding and road safety test, designed to teach participants to ride with safety and courtesy and comply with the *Highway Code*. The test is divided into three parts; part one is theory, part two is a simulated road test and part three is carried out in real road conditions.

Before you even think of venturing out on the road, make sure that pony and rider are properly equipped. The pony must be properly tacked up (never ride bareback or in a headcollar) and his tack and shoes must be in good condition. The rider, of course, must wear a properly fitted BSI standard hat and suitable footwear, and it is a good idea to make sure that she has money for the phone in case of emergency. Duvaxyn rider cards, available free from your vet, are another good safety idea. These are filled in with the rider's name, 'phone number and any medical conditions or allergies, and secured to the hat lining.

There is also the question of insurance. Hopefully you will already have your pony insured, but check that your policy includes third party legal liability insurance. There are circumstances in which you could be held liable for damage to people or property caused by your pony, and it may prove expensive.

A pony should always be ridden or led on the left hand side of the road. If he is being led the person in charge of him should be on his right hand side (offside) so that he is between the pony and the traffic, thus giving the leader more control.

Going for a hack is a nice way of relaxing pony and rider, but you cannot afford to relax too much. It is vital to stay alert and aware of road conditions –

and like any other road user, you should check it is safe before making any manoeuvre and signal your intention to do so first. Clear hand signals are vital – it is no good a rider making vague waves at a motorist and expecting him to understand what she means.

Courtesy and safety go hand in hand, and all riders should make an effort to smile and thank drivers who slow down for them. If the pony is anxious and the rider cannot take a hand off the reins to signal her thanks she can still smile and nod her appreciation. Unfortunately one ignorant rider can give the rest a bad name, and some children take courteous drivers for granted. If you pull over to make room for a rider and your courtesy goes unnoticed, why not make a point of drawing the rider's attention to it? Politely pointing out that such lack of courtesy is not going to encourage drivers to be considerate to other riders often works wonders.

Many riders are confused about how close they should ride to the edge of the road. The answer is as close as is safe, but you need to take particular conditions into account. For instance, if you are riding along a narrow road with overhanging hedges, it can be safer to move out towards the centre of the road so that approaching vehicles can see you. In the same way, I would recommend moving out a little to prevent drivers trying to overtake where there is not enough room for it to be safe, pulling into a passing place as soon as possible.

It is important that pony and rider are visible, especially if they have to ride out in bad weather. Riding clothes are traditionally dark in colour, and a bay pony ridden by a rider in black hat and green jacket merges frighteningly well with the hedge. Where possible, stay off the roads when visibility is bad, especially when it is getting dark, but if you do have to ride or lead in these conditions make sure you can be seen.

There are many excellent visibility aids on the market now, ranging from reflective fluorescent belts and tabards for riders to leg bands for horses. Research has shown that these have a great impact on motorists and prompt them to slow down to a much greater degree than they would for a rider in ordinary clothes, so kit out your pony and rider – pony leg bands and rider belt or tabard are the most effective combination.

If your daughter goes out for a ride with one or more friends they need to keep their collective wits about them. Where necessary, they should ride in single file, but if a pony gets agitated it can help to put a quiet, steady animal on his outside. Crossing roads can be a hazard, and, whenever possible, the group should cross at the same time to avoid ponies worrying about being left behind and trying to pull out into the road to catch up with the others.

Reflective fluorescent belts, tabards and leg bands

Everyone has favourite hacks, but it is important to vary routes so that the pony does not get into the habit of, say, always turning left out the drive and right at the end of the road. Always taking the same route, or going for a ride and then turning round and retracing your steps, can encourage nappiness, a behavioural problem where the pony refuses to go where you want him to (see the chapter on problems). And while it is tempting to make the most of that lovely canter along a bridleway, it is a good idea to walk sometimes so that the rider is the one who dictates the pace, not the pony. Finally, make sure that when your daughter sets off on a hack someone at the yard knows her proposed route. You then know where to look if she is so late back you suspect some sort of accident.

Most accidents do not happen at competitive events when riders are jumping fences at speed. They happen while people are riding purely for pleasure, and the most common form of pleasure riding is hacking. Research by Dr Michael

Whitlock, an expert in accident and emergency services, showed that 68.6 per cent of all riding accidents involved riding purely for pleasure – and a quarter happen whilst the horse is at walk. Here is a checklist for safe riding:

- Check that rider and pony are properly equipped. Worn or badly fitting tack or loose shoes can cause accidents. Riders should always wear a hat complying with BSI standards, and the hat harness should always be fastened.
- Boots with hard soles and small heels should be worn. Trainers and wellingtons with ridged soles are dangerous.
- Make sure the rider can be seen. In bad weather or poor light the rider should wear a fluorescent reflective belt or tabard and the pony should have leg bands in the same material.
- Anyone forced to ride at night (and it should be avoided whenever possible) must wear a reflective stirrup light showing white to the front and red to the rear. When leading a horse at night, wear reflective clothing and carry a light showing white to the front and red to the rear.
- When riding in a group, experienced riders should be at the front and rear of the ride, with the less experienced riders in between.
- Always ride on the left, singly or in pairs. There is nothing wrong with riding two abreast if this is to ensure that an inexperienced or nervous horse is kept on the inside or to prevent drivers overtaking where there is insufficient room. However, try to keep in single file where possible on narrow roads and bends.
- Do not ride so close to the kerb that drivers cannot see you, for instance on a road bordered by a hedge, but be careful that cyclists do not try to overtake between the pony and the kerb.
- Anticipation and observation are vital. Look round before moving off or moving out, to overtake a parked car for example, then listen, look again and signal correctly.
- Always thank drivers who slow down or stop. A nod and a smile will do if you cannot take your hands off the reins.
- The rider should be competent enough and the pony well-schooled enough to ensure that proper control can be maintained. The rider should turn the pony's head away from frightening things but use her legs to keep him straight – if she cannot do this, riding lessons are called for. Every rider should carry a whip on the roads to reinforce leg aids if necessary.
- If leading a pony on the road, put his bridle on and lead on the left, keeping yourself between him and the traffic. Again, it is a good idea to carry a whip.

- Remember that shows and other competitions are busy places with lots of traffic. Apply the same safety guidelines here as to riding on the road.

Security

Ponies and their equipment are expensive. This means, unfortunately, that horse and tack theft is big business – so make sure that you do not provide thieves with easy pickings. The financial loss is bad enough, but you cannot put a price on the heartbreak of losing a pony. *Horse and Hound* regularly carries details of stolen animals; some are recovered but others end up being sold for meat.

Horse thieves, like burglars, go for the easy victims; why bother with the field with post and rail fencing, overlooked by a house, when you can visit the lonely one down the road and cut through the wire fence? Security is an issue that must be kept in mind when finding somewhere to keep your pony, even if it has to be added to lots of other considerations. If you are renting land you have to make do with the best you can get, but good stout fencing and padlocked metal gates that cannot be lifted off their hinges are a safety bonus. All field gates should, in any case, be padlocked; people might tell you it is a waste of time if a thief can simply take a pair of wire cutters to your fence, but a padlock will at least deter vandals – some of whom get peculiar pleasure from letting ponies out of their fields. Padlocks are not a good idea for individual stables, though, as they can hamper or even prevent rescue in the case of a fire.

If you want impartial, expert and free advice on the best way to protect your premises, contact the crime prevention officer at your local police station. He or she will arrange to visit you and suggest ways that your security can be improved.

Freeze Marking

The best protection you can give your pony is to have him freeze marked; a company called Premier FarmKey based in Banbury, Oxon, has a nationwide team of operators and co-operates with police forces throughout the UK. So far all stolen animals freeze marked by this company have been returned to their owners.

Freeze marking is a painless process carried out by a skilled operator used to handling horses, and is a definite deterrent to thieves. Often organised gangs will go to a yard, take the horses' rugs off and take only unmarked animals.

Ignore people who tell you that freeze marking is cruel, or that it will lead to you getting marked down in the show ring. If it hurt the pony he would tell you so in no uncertain terms; I have seen it done several times and, without exception, the animals have been no more than wary. The person doing the job uses little 'branding irons' that have been chemically frozen to mark the animal with his own personal code. The chemicals kill off the cells in the skin that make pigment, so the hair grows back white – or with grey horses, does not grow back at all. It takes about five minutes to freeze mark a pony and at first the code shows up as swellings on the skin. These then turn to scabs, which flake off, and the hair grows back in five or six weeks. A freeze marked pony can be ridden a few days after the process has been done; the operator will tell you how long to wait.

The pony is usually freeze marked under the saddle, so when he is being ridden it does not show at all. In the case of grey ponies, the freeze marked area needs to be kept clipped in winter so the thick coat does not hide it. Occa-

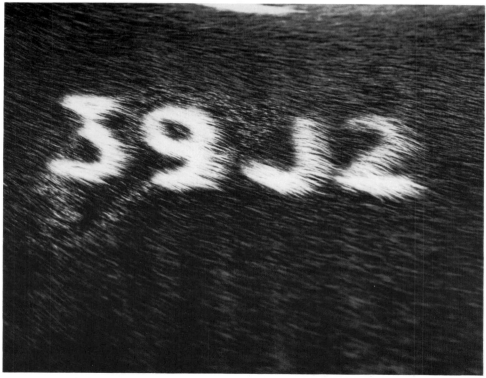

A freeze mark is a good way of deterring would-be horse thieves

sionally a mark does not take properly, because the operator has to gauge how many seconds to hold the iron on for according to the pony's colour and type. In this case, it will be redone free of charge.

Freeze marking is not expensive when you think of the protection it gives your pony, and it is even cheaper if more than one animal is done at the same time. Sometimes riding schools and clubs organise freeze marking sessions, or you could team up with other owners in your area to set up one of your own. Once your pony has been marked the freeze marking company will enter his details on a central register, and if he is stolen they will be circulated to all horse sales and slaughter houses. No scrupulous slaughter company will destroy an animal without ensuring that the person who authorises the slaughter is the rightful owner. Similarly, no trustworthy auctioneer would let a freeze marked pony go through the ring if the person who entered it in the sale did not have the freeze mark papers.

If the worst comes to the worst and he is stolen before you have had the chance to get him freeze marked, contact the police and as many horse sales and slaughter houses as you can; the British Horse Society can provide you with a list in return for a stamped addressed envelope. Do not just concentrate on local ones, because organised gangs steal horses one day and have them at the other end of the country in a few hours. There have even been cases of thieves doing a reconnaissance in a particular area, deciding which animals they are going to steal and entering them at sales a long way away. Then at the last minute they move in, carry out the thefts and take the animals to auction.

Another good security tip is to take colour photographs of your pony in his summer and winter coats, preferably from several angles to show any markings such as blazes or socks. Make a note of any permanent identifying marks, such as scars, and if he is kept at livery make sure the yard owner or manager has copies of your documentation. When a pony is stolen, speed is vital.

Tack and Rug Security

Having your tack stolen is obviously not as traumatic as losing your pony, but it is still an unpleasant and expensive experience. Do not be complacent and think that because you have your tack insured the insurance company will pay out; they will, but only if you comply with their terms to the last letter. Most insist, for instance, that tackrooms must be locked at all times – yet how many yards or riding schools can do this? On a busy weekend, with people coming in and out all the time, it just is not practical to lock the door every time a set of tack is taken out or put away.

If you can, keep tack at home in the house (and get the local crime prevention officer to check your security there, too). Mark it with your postcode so that if it is stolen and you recognise it being offered for sale, or it is recovered, you can identify it. You can either use the FarmKey tack marking system or do it yourself using one of the readily available engraving 'pens' on metal and an ultra violet pen on the underside of leather. Mark bits, buckles and stirrup bars with the engraving pen, and bridle pieces, saddle flaps and girth guards with the ultra violet one (which only shows up when an ultra violet light is shone on it and needs renewing regularly; check the manufacturer's instructions). Many police forces now hold regular marking sessions where you can take your tack along to be marked free of charge.

Every now and again there seem to be spates of rugs being stolen literally from horses' backs. Thieves take New Zealand rugs off ponies in the fields to sell at auction and leave the poor animals shivering and their owners poorer by the cost of a new rug. Discourage this by permanently marking each rug with your initials in letters so big would-be thieves cannot fail to notice them.

Discourage would-be rug thieves

14 Transporting the Pony

One of the nicest things about having a pony in the family is that you soon make friends with others in the same situation. It will not take long for your daughter to find others to ride with, and then she will want to join in shows, sponsored rides and all the other enjoyable activities that take up your weekends and eat up any spare cash you might have managed to scrimp and save. Make joining the local Pony Club branch top of your list of things to do, because your daughter will learn the right way to ride and look after her pony and be able to join in rallies and competitions. You can even get a bit of peace and quiet by packing her off to Pony Club camp in the summer holidays! If you do not know where the nearest branch is, write to Pony Club headquarters at the British Equestrian Centre, Stoneleigh, Kenilworth, Warwickshire CV8 2LR.

Many events will be within hacking distance, but the day is bound to come when you want to go farther afield and have to arrange transport. You might be lucky to find someone kind and capable who will give your pony a lift in their lorry or trailer; if so, remember that boxes are expensive to run and towing a trailer may add to car maintenance costs and increase petrol consumption. Offering to pay for all, or at least half of the fuel costs will be appreciated, even if your Good Samaritan is so rich he can afford to be magnanimous.

If you cannot find someone with space for your pony, the other alternatives are to hire or buy your own transport. If you can afford to go out and buy a horsebox (truck), you are very fortunate; a good small secondhand one will cost about the same as a new small car. For most families this is out of the question, not just because of the money but because of finding somewhere secure to park the box when it is not in use.

Hiring Transport

Hiring a box and driver from a specialist horse transport firm can be the best idea if a group of you get together. It is too expensive to do alone, because hiring a box for a day at a local show will probably cost £50–£60 plus VAT, although when you consider that this includes fuel costs, depreciation costs on the box and the driver's time and skills, it is good value for money. If three or four of you get together it means you end up paying about £15–£25 each. The main disadvantage of hiring is that unless you are super efficient and book well in advance you might find that demand is so heavy, especially in the show season, that someone else has beaten you to it. The best way is to find a firm that suits you (word of mouth recommendations are the best ones) and to become one of their 'regulars'. That way they are more likely to try and fit you in during the busy times.

Be prepared to pay a non-refundable deposit when you book a box, usually about £10, and be specific about where you want to go and what time you want to arrive. An experienced driver will then allow enough time for easy loading: if one of the ponies is known to sometimes be a reluctant loader, be honest and tell him. It is unlikely he will refuse your booking, but he will be able to allow extra time for problems. As the chapter on problems explains, most loading difficulties are caused by bad handling, and a professional transporter with time and patience can often help cure them.

To avoid any misunderstandings, check when you make your booking whether there are any surcharges after a certain time and whether the firm makes you its sole booking for the day or expects to make another journey as well. Some transporters add a surcharge for every hour they are out after, say, half past five and may expect to take two parties to a show if one is competing in morning classes and the other in afternoon ones. Personally, I like to know that if I have hired a box it is mine for the day. That way you have a base on the showground and know you can put the ponies in the box in between classes if it is raining. You can also be sure that you can leave exactly when you want to, instead of having to hang about while the driver takes the other group home first.

On a purely financial basis, you will find that as long as there are enough of you to make it worthwhile, hiring is a lot cheaper than buying your own transport, unless you are going to be here, there and everywhere every weekend. Even then hiring might work out cheaper – although you do not have the opportunity of being able to go somewhere on the off chance. Financial considerations aside, every horse and pony owner dreams of owning their own transport.

Trailers

If you decide to buy your own transport, a trailer is the cheapest form. Remember that trailers have to be parked when not in use, preferably under cover in the winter, and on ground where it is possible to tow them off in wet going.

Your choice of towing vehicle is as important as your choice of trailer. Ignore people who tell you that your family car will tow anything, because the chances are that it will not. A general guideline is to combine the largest, most powerful car you can afford (four-wheel drive is a real bonus) with the smallest trailer that comfortably meets your pony's needs. Then work out your priorities, of which the pony's safety and comfort must come first.

All car manufacturers give recommended towing weights. Some people, including trailer manufacturers, might tell you that these are over-cautious – but stick to them. They are there for your and your pony's safety. The car manufacturers' figures are based on a driver being able to restart on a 12 per cent gradient at sea level, and there is a big difference between what your car is capable of towing on a level road and what it is safe to tow. After all, do you really want to find out that you have been over-optimistic when you are going down a hill?

Towing experts at the Caravan Club advise that the general aim should be to tow a weight that is no more than 85 per cent of the car's kerb weight (off-road vehicles are an exception). They organise nationwide courses to teach drivers how to tow and will also give impartial advice on towing: contact them on 0342 326944. If you want to know what your car is capable of, you should also be able to get information about kerb and maximum towing weights from the manufacturers or the Caravan Club.

At current prices, you will be able to buy a new trailer for around £2,000. Basic prices usually include all you need, though you might want to invest in extras like rubber matting on the floor. Front unload trailers are slightly heavier and inevitably more expensive than simple rear unload kinds, though if you are careful and the pony is calm to unload you can save money by going for rear unload only. Do not, however, be tempted to buy a single horse trailer. They are never as stable as the double ones, and you will probably need the extra space at some time.

There are, of course, perfectly good secondhand trailers available; they often come on the market because children lost interest in ponies or the family buys a horsebox as commitment and finances increase. It must be said that a horsebox will, nine times out of ten, give a pony a better ride than a trailer, but obviously any form of transport is only as good as its driver. If you buy a secondhand trailer, get it checked over by someone knowledgeable first; faulty brakes can land you in hospital, and in court, and there are other regulations about lights, etc., that must be adhered to. One of the best ways to buy second-hand is to buy a reconditioned, warranted model from a recognised trailer dealer – they often take them in part-exchange when people trade up.

Whether you buy a new trailer or a secondhand one, remember it needs regular maintenance. Lights, tyres and wheel nuts should be checked every week as a matter of course, whether the trailer has been used or not. Once a month, take up any flooring and check the floor for any signs of rot or damage – there have been some horrific accidents when horses have put their feet through rotten floors. Finally, book your trailer in for a full service and maintenance by your nearest manufacturer-appointed dealer at least once a year. He will check brakes, coupling, lights, floors and ramps and carry out necessary repairs.

Once you have bought your trailer, protect it from thieves. Trailer theft is big business, so whenever possible park it somewhere that is overlooked and fit a security device such as a wheel clamp or hitch lock. Several firms specialise in marking trailers with registration numbers that are impossible to remove, but you should also have a security device to make it very difficult for anyone else to hitch-up your trailer. It may be hard to believe, but there have actually been cases of thieves driving on to showgrounds, hitching up trailers and towing them off while the owners are competing!

Towing a Trailer

If you are wondering why I have left the subject of loading the pony until last, the reason is that a lot of preparation is needed beforehand. You might hear of people who have never towed a trailer before buying one one day, then loading up the pony and going to a show the next. They are an accident waiting to happen: do not follow their example.

Most experience transporters say that once you are used to the difference in size, boxes are easier to drive than trailers are to tow. But whatever you have bought, practise driving without the pony to start with. If you have to collect the trailer yourself, try and find a friend who will let you practise towing theirs first (preferably off-road to start with). Most manufacturers are only too aware of the dangers of a driver who has not towed before, and will give purchasers a quick lesson before letting them take the trailer home.

Basically, you have to take a lot of time over all changes in movement. Do not accelerate or brake suddenly or turn through corners fast. Do not accelerate through corners as hard as you would when driving a car. Watch out for changes in camber; for instance, on roundabouts the camber leans in, but when you leave the roundabout it might go a completely different way. Remember, too, that other drivers might not use their common sense and realise that you need to go slower and wider round corners and bends than a car on its own: be prepared for the ones who try to cut inside. As you have probably guessed, you need to react earlier than you would when driving normally. Slamming on the brakes at the last minute will upset your four-legged passenger and, at worst, could make the trailer jack-knife.

Reversing is the part which most people dread, but if you keep calm and manoeuvre slowly you should be all right. Start off with trailer and towing vehicle in a straight line, and if you have a choice, reverse to the right – it is easier to see what is happening on the driver's side because you can check out of the window. If you reverse to the left, you have to make good use of your wing mirror; both wing mirrors should be properly adjusted before you set off on any journey.

I could not understand reversing with a trailer until someone pointed out to me that when you tow a trailer you are pulling it, and when you reverse you are pushing it. Suddenly there was light at the end of the tunnel! Assuming that you are reversing to the right and are positioned in a straight line, start reversing very slowly, turning the steering wheel slightly to the left. As the trailer goes right on to the line you want it to follow, gently adjust the steering wheel so that your towing vehicle follows it. If you reverse to the left, start by turning the wheel right, being extra careful because you are having to rely on your wing mirror. Remember that the golden rules are to go slowly and to make small corrections to the steering – if the trailer starts to jackknife, drive forwards and start again.

The most frightening thing that can happen when you are towing is for the trailer to start snaking. High winds are a common cause, so when in doubt, stay at home. If you do get caught out, experts recommend that you should take your foot off the accelerator and let the vehicle slow down on its own. Do not try to steer your way out of it, because you will probably make things worse; let the wheel 'twitch' in your hand, try to keep a straight course and accelerate gently.

The best and most experienced horse transporter I know, who travels horses ranging from children's ponies to extremely valuable bloodstock, says that he wishes more people who owned trailers would take them on to private ground and ride in them while someone else does the towing. They would then understand what their horses experience and might take more care. It is illegal, by the way, to travel in a trailer on the roads – so do not ever be tempted to let your daughter keep the pony company.

It is always worthwhile planning your route beforehand, because the quickest way in a car is not always the quickest way when towing a trailer. A longer route but with wider, straighter roads can be easier on the clock and the nerves. If you are only transporting one pony in a double trailer you should put him on the right side (offside), to help counteract the effect of road camber. Finally, do not follow the example of one dedicated Pony Club family I know. Tack and show gear was stowed in the back, the pony was kitted out in his travelling gear and the picnic was on the back seat. Off they went, and arrived at the showground. It was only when they parked and went to check the pony that they realised they had forgotten to load him and had left him ready and waiting in his stable!

Preparing the Pony

For happy, stress-free travelling you need to stick to three golden rules; plenty of room, plenty of air and plenty of time for preparation. A pony who is worried or tired by his journey obviously is not going to be very happy when he gets there. Some animals are labelled 'bad travellers' but it is inevitably people who have made them that way.

Before you load the pony make sure that the box or trailer is adequately ventilated but not too draughty and make sure that he has enough room. A pony spreads his feet to keep his balance and is more comfortable that way. Many problems with trailers are caused by people moving the partition nearer the pony because they think it will give him support and he will be more comfortable. In fact, the reverse is true. Good flooring with straw or shavings put down gives him stability and makes it easier to clean out the trailer when you get home; never clean out on a showground or car park, it is antisocial.

Your pony needs to be protected with special clothing for travelling so that he does not knock or cut himself as he shifts to keep his balance. For safety's sake, use a leather headcollar as opposed to a nylon one; leather will break in an emergency but nylon will not. As at home, tie him to a piece of string which is in turn attached to the metal ring, not to the ring itself, and give him a haynet to keep him happy on the journey.

RUGS

The sort of rug you use depends on the weather, your pony's natural coat and how draughty or otherwise the vehicle is. You might find in summer that he does not need a rug at all for short journeys, while in winter he will need to be kept warm. No matter how warm it is when you set off, always take a sweat rug and a light rug or summer sheet to put over the top of it. At the end of the day, when he is tired, he might break out in a sweat again even after he has cooled off. A sweat rug topped by a light rug with the sides folded back, held in place with a roller, will prevent this. If your rug only has a surcingle, buy a special pad from your saddler that ensures there is no pressure on the pony's spine.

BOOTS AND BANDAGES

It is vital to protect your pony's legs with either boots or bandages. Both have their advantages and disadvantages: boots are quick and easy to put on and take off, but they can slip and rub. Bandages are more fiddly, but if put on properly give support as well as protection. Some of the specially designed travelling boots cover the knees and hocks, but if you buy short boots or use bandages you will need to use knee and hock boots as well. It might sound like a lot of fuss and bother, but it is all too easy for a pony to bang himself, especially if he gets impatient or even kicks out.

Boots usually fasten with Velcro and should be put on so that the fastenings point to the pony's tail. Bandages should be applied over gamgee or washable bandage pads (the latter are much more economical because they can be re-used). Make sure that your bandages are rolled with the tapes to the inside, then wrap the padding round and keep hold of it. This is where parents often have to help, as small fingers can't manage it. Bandage the legs as described in Chapter 11.

Even if you use boots you cannot get out of bandaging completely. A tail bandage is essential even for short journeys, both to stop your pony rubbing the hair and to protect the bones at the top. Tail bandages are about three inches wide, and because they are elasticated should never be dampened; as they dry they constrict, and can hamper circulation, with terrible effects, so dampen the hair but never the bandage.

Again, start by checking that the bandage is rolled with the tapes to the inside. Place the bandage underneath the tail as high as you can, leaving a few inches overlap. Some ponies are very obliging and will lift their tails slightly, making the job much easier, while others clamp them down tightly, If your pony objects, be patient; try tickling the skin underneath the dock. Once you have made the first turn, fold the overlap down and bandage over it. I like to make two or three turns at the top, to give more protection to the most vulnerable area, and you can then continue down the tail until all the bones are

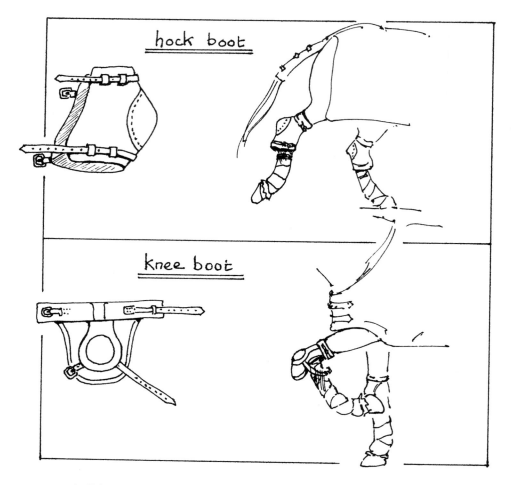

covered. Then either tie the tapes or bandage them back up the tail again, depending on how much bandage if left. It is important that the tapes are tied securely, but do not use a knot so complicated you cannot undo it – I like a double bow – then tuck the tapes in and fold a piece of the bandage over them. Finally, gently bend the tail back into position.

There is a knack to removing leg bandages (as described in Chapter 10) and tail bandages. To remove a tail bandage, undo the tapes then grasp the bandage firmly at the top with both hands and pull down. It will simply slide off and

Small fingers can't manage it

you can then roll it up again. Life is much more pleasant, by the way, if you take spare leg and tail bandages. Rolling up soggy, dirty ones so you can put them on again is not a pleasant task.

Knee and hock boots should be fastened so that the top straps are tight enough to just admit one finger and the bottom ones are much looser. Remember that the pony needs to be able to flex his joints while wearing them. When you remove knee or hock boots, always undo the bottom strap first – if you undo the top strap first, the boots will slip down and irritate or even frighten the pony.

If your pony throws his head up while travelling, add a poll guard as a final protective measure. This is a pad with slots for the headcollar to pass through which protects the sensitive poll area between his ears.

When he is all dressed and ready to go, park the box or trailer on level ground so that the ramp is stable when lowered. In theory, you should be able to lead him straight up the ramp, but not all ponies are so obliging.

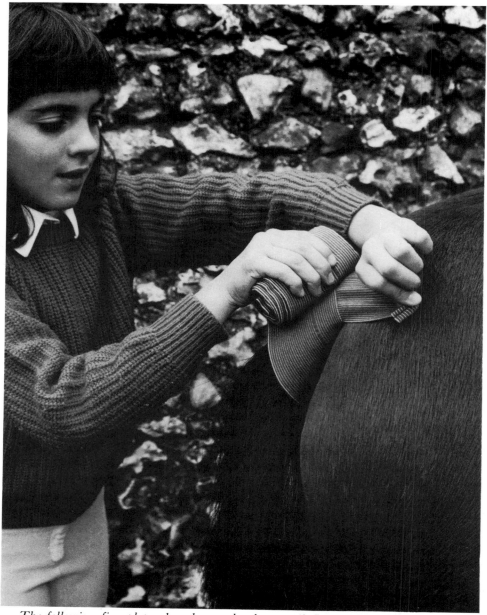

The following five plates show how to bandage a tail. Leave a short flap at the top.

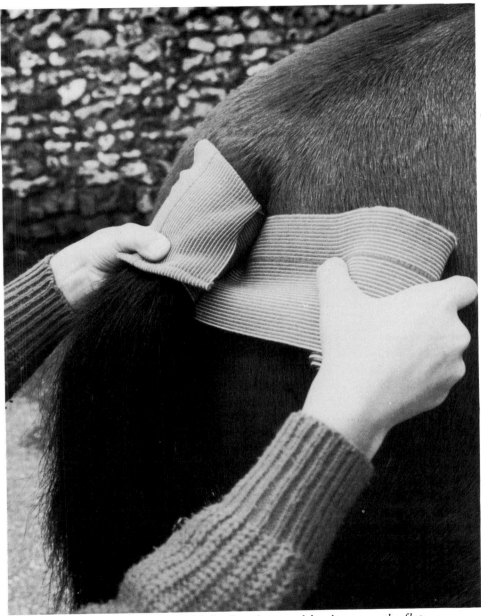

After the first turn, fold the flap down and bandage over the flap.

Continue to the end of the dock.

Bandage back up the tail and tie the tapes. Fold a layer of bandage over the tapes and tuck the loose ends away.

Gently bend the bandaged tail back into position so that it lies comfortably.

The Reluctant Loader

Nothing is more infuriating than a pony who refuses to go into a trailer or horsebox. Do not blame the pony, however, blame the people who have made him reluctant. Bad handling and bad driving make bad travellers, just as quiet loading and the prospect of a comfortable journey result in a pony who walks cheerfully up the ramp.

Check that you are doing your bit right. Make sure the interior is light enough for the pony to see where he is going, then stand at his shoulder and lead him in a straight line towards it. Without looking back or pulling, walk in ahead of him. Tie him up straight away and in the case of a trailer get someone to fasten the breeching strap behind him.

A professional transporter

If your pony has never been in a vehicle before, let him have a good look at it with the ramp down. Over the next few days feed him by putting the bucket on the ramp, gradually moving it up so that he stands on the ramp and eventually goes inside. Unload him carefully and quietly, keeping him in a straight line.

You can cure a bad loader on your own, if you have enough time, patience and confidence, but you will be far better off getting expert help – and I mean expert, not someone who thinks the best thing to do is shove a prickly yard broom up the pony's backside. The shock might make it work the first time, but you are likely to have even more trouble the next. It is a good idea to invest in hiring a professional transporter for the afternoon; ask around for someone who is known for being patient and efficient. If you explain that you have a difficult loader his experience will probably enable him to solve the problem for you.

One transporter tells the story of a mare who was 'impossible' to load. Her owners called him out in desperation, and he realised that the reason she would not go in was that the interior of the box was badly lit. Presented with his light, well-ventilated vehicle and a confident handler, she walked straight up the ramp.

If you are forced to cope alone, follow his example and stay calm. If the pony walks up to the ramp then hesitates, do not turn him straight away. Talk to him and let him have a look and he might decide it is worth a go. If you have no joy, calmly turn away, walk a couple of circles and present him at the ramp again.

If he still says no, you will need two helpers and two lunge reins. Fasten each rein to the back of the vehicle, about halfway up, and get each helper to hold them straight out. Lead the pony up to the ramp and get the helpers to cross over behind him so that the lunge reins cross just above his hocks. Usually the pressure will encourage him to walk forwards and up the ramp. A variation on this theme is for two people to link hands behind the pony, just above his hocks, and gently push forwards – but be careful in case he kicks.

Occasionally a pony will refuse to load out of sheer naughtiness. If you are sure this is the case, and only if you are sure, a slap with a stick is in order. A dealer who has never yet been beaten by problem ponies also recommends flicking at the pony's heels with a lunge whip, which will not hurt but will irritate him. Do be sure to keep well out of range of possible kicks, and stop flicking as soon as he starts walking up the ramp.

15 The Problem Pony

No matter how carefully you look after your pony, things will not always go the way you want them to. But while problems can be exasperating and in the worst cases even frightening, learning how to solve them is one of the fascinations of being a pony owner. You can minimise problems by getting to know your pony and, therefore, being able to spot straight away when something is not right, and by thinking ahead – for instance, making sure your daughter has regular lessons with a good instructor will mean the pony is less likely to develop bad habits. Even so, there will be times when a situation arises that you do not know how to cope with. This chapter is designed to give you an insight into some of the most common problems and to provide some tried and tested ways of dealing with them – but as every pony is an individual, what works for one might not be as successful with another.

There is nothing worse than struggling alone; never be afraid to ask for advice, but be sure that the person you seek it from knows what they are talking about. If what is suggested makes sense, act on it. Do not ask half a dozen other people what they think, because you will probably end up with several suggestions and will be so confused you will not know what to do. Equally, do not be frightened of looking stupid. Everyone is a novice owner to start with, and it is far more sensible to ask questions than to take pot luck and risk doing the wrong thing.

Most behavioural and riding problems start in a small way. It is when they are ignored in the hope that they will go away – which they will not – that they turn into real headaches. So remember to be consistent in the way you handle your pony; be reasonable, but expect good manners from him and correct him if he does not show them.

Hopefully you will have started off with a well-mannered, obedient pony. If you treat him the right way, he should stay that way; many problems are

The pony is less likely to develop bad habits

caused by riders and handlers, however inadvertently, so make sure that neither you nor your daughter are to blame. Analyse the problem; if the pony has started refusing to jump, is your daughter jumping him so much that he is sick of it, or is she catching him in the mouth as he takes off? A pony will not carry on doing something that hurts him. Similarly, if he suddenly starts snatching at the bit or opening his mouth it could be that the bit is the wrong size or not properly adjusted, or that his teeth are sharp.

There are three vital first steps to dealing with a riding problem – get someone knowledgeable to check the pony, check the fit and condition of his tack and check your daughter's riding. Nine times out of ten, these will reveal the cause of the problem; if they do not, you need professional help to persuade the pony of the error of his ways. In most cases your instructor will be able to help your daughter 'ride through' the problem, but sometimes a more experienced rider may be needed.

Difficult to Catch

A friend of mine says that you do not appreciate a horse or pony that is good to catch until you own one that is not. Her mare is fine during the autumn and winter, but in spring and summer decides she would rather stay out and enjoy the nice grass. My friend knows the mare so well that she can guess by her general behaviour when the problem is going to start and can take evasive action – which ranges from putting her in a tiny paddock to visiting her with titbits on occasions when she does not want to catch her and bring her in.

It is a good idea to sometimes catch your pony, give him a treat, check him over and let him go again. If he automatically associates being caught with being ridden, he will keep well out of your way, but if there is a chance that he might just get a carrot and a pat, he could be more sociable. It will also be easier to catch a clever pony if you leave a leather headcollar on him with a piece of rope about a foot long attached (it is worth sacrificing a leadrope). When he has accepted the titbit, gently take hold of the rope. Never be tempted to grab, because although it might work the first time he will be wise to it the next time. It is easier to get hold of the piece of rope than trying to get hold of the head-collar.

Ponies are gregarious and curious, both traits that can be turned to your advantage. If your pony is turned out with other ponies, ask their owners if you can catch them first. It is time consuming if you have to catch, and later turn out again, two ponies to get your own, but can be quicker in the long run. Some ponies that are hard to catch become as meek as anything when they realise that they are going to be left on their own in the field.

Another trick that sometimes works is to go into the field and wander round as if you are looking for something. Ignore the pony to start with, then gradually bring your 'search' closer to him. Do not look at him, just get nearer and nearer until you are able to offer him a titbit. Walk away again; if he follows you in the hope of another, so much the better, but if he does not, casually stroll back to him. Give him another treat and gently take hold of the cut-off leadrope as before.

If none of these methods work, you will have to take drastic action. Turn the pony out in a field with no water and take a bucketful with you a few hours later. If he lets you catch him, make a fuss of him and let him drink. If not, take the water away. You might feel awful about it, but he will not come to any harm on the first day. Visit him again a couple of hours later, but stick to your guns – no catching, no water. If this goes on into the second day, you will have to make your visits more frequent. Eventually the pony will be so thirsty that he will be eager to be caught, and you can let him drink. Do not, however, let him gulp down gallons of water all in one go; offer half to three-quarters of a bucket at regular intervals. All being well, the lesson will have been learnt and you can give him back his water supply. Remember to make regular visits; when you catch him, give him a titbit and then let him go and you should be all right. *It must be emphasised that this method must only be used as a last resort.*

Some people might advise you to tether a pony that is difficult to catch, but this is not advisable. It is too easy for a pony to become tangled in the tethering rope and there have been cases of animals strangling themselves.

Tacking Up

If a pony takes a dislike to being tacked up, it is usually because he has been made to feel uncomfortable, so double-check that he is being tacked up correctly. A small child who cannot manage alone should have adult help.

Remember that there may also be physical reasons for the pony's disquiet when being bridled and saddled; a sore mouth – the teeth may need attention – a sore back, girth galls or rubs – from badly fitting tack, poor riding or skin being pinched by the girth. Once you are sure the tack fits correctly, and the pony has been checked by the vet and pronounced sound, you may still have to deal with the pony's remaining fear or dislike of being tacked up.

If your pony has been made to resent the process of bridling so much that he throws his head up and is totally uncooperative, you will have to take a step backwards in order to put things right. Remove the reins and fasten the bit to the right cheekpiece only. Put the bridle over the pony's head, keeping hold of the bit so that it does not hit him, then tickle his tongue as before. When he opens his mouth, slip the bit in, fasten the other cheekpiece, and replace the reins.

When putting the saddle on do so gently, then make sure that everything is in the correct place, with the numnah and coat lying correctly. When the girth is tightened, pull each foreleg forwards to ensure that the skin under the girth is not wrinkled and being pinched.

Untacking can be equally traumatic for the pony if handled roughly, so take just as much care when doing this.

Shying

Most ponies shy at some time or other, either because they have been genuinely startled by something or because they are feeling a bit silly. If the pony is generally bouncing around and acting the fool, make sure he is not getting too much high protein food. Oats in particular can have a mind-blowing effect on ponies, so check that no one is misguidedly adding a few to his feed to try and liven him up. Not surprisingly, frosty or windy weather makes some ponies more excitable, so if your pony is one who literally gets the wind under his tail, play safe. High winds make it more difficult to hear approaching traffic and can also blow paper bags and litter in front of the pony just at the wrong moment.

If both these causes have been eliminated, correct riding is the answer. In theory the pony should be well schooled enough for your daughter to be able to slightly turn his head away from the object that is making him spook and use her legs to make him go past. If one or both of them does not understand, it is time for more riding lessons.

Never hit a pony for shying, even if you are sure he is doing it out of sheer devilment. Hitting him will reinforce the idea that there is something to be frightened of, and if he starts to associate being frightened of paper bags, for example, with being hit, you will make the problem worse.

The big problem about spooking and shying is that the rider has to stay alert and ready to take evasive action but at the same time remain relaxed. If she tenses up, the pony will sense it and become even more wary. It is all too easy for the rider to assume that the pony is going to shy at a plastic bag in the hedgerow, and take a firmer grip on the reins, but, again, all this will do is make him think there *is* something to be frightened of. If shying becomes a habit, get experienced help and ask your vet to check the pony's eyesight.

Napping

Nothing is worse than a nappy pony or horse that decides it does not want to go where you want it to and has a repertoire of tricks to try and avoid it. In an ideal world you should never give in to a nappy animal, but if a pony naps for the first time when your daughter is on her own she might give up and come home. Write that one off as the pony's victory, and make sure it does not happen again. If a couple of good smacks do not persuade the pony to move forwards, your daughter should turn him in several tight circles – so tight that he is turning in his own length – then straighten him without warning and drive him on with legs and stick. Sometimes a nappy pony will run backwards, which can be disconcerting for the rider. If it is safe to do so, keep him going backwards, and when he has decided he has made his point and wants to go forwards, then kick him on again.

If all else fails, there is one last, highly irregular ploy. Put an experienced rider on board and head for the quietest roads you can find, following on behind in a car with a passenger armed with a lunge whip. As soon as the pony starts to nap the driver (who should at all times keep the car at a safe distance) pulls over and the passenger leaps out with the lunge whip. Brandishing it might be enough, but the shock of lunge whip meeting pony's backside usually has the desired effect. Do be careful, though, that the person with the lunge whip is skilful enough not to wrap it round the pony's legs or hit the rider.

Napping is something a pony learns, so try not to let him. It is asking for trouble if you always take the same route or worse still, go so far then turn back and retrace your steps. While it is nice to hack out in company, your pony should not be allowed to get into the habit of always following another pony; he too should take his turn in the lead.

Most ponies who nap simply plant their feet firmly on the ground and refuse to move, but occasionally – and fortunately few ponies develop this vice – they may rear.

Rearing

A pony who rears habitually is not a safe mount for a child and should be reschooled by someone with a good deal of experience of this problem. If the pony cannot be cured then, in my view, he should be put down; could you honestly take the risk of selling him knowing that he could endanger another child's life?

I once had a talented horse who was a brilliant jumper and kindness itself in the stable, but take him out on the roads on his own and he would suddenly decide he was not going any further. His evasion was to try and spin round, then rear and plunge forwards. Eventually we cured him to the extent that as long as he had a strong rider with quick reactions he would behave, but as soon as anyone less experienced rode him, he would try his old tricks again.

Bucking

Some ponies occasionally throw a buck when they are feeling well and happy, and there is nothing wrong with this – all you have to do is make sure that your daughter can stay on! The best way to sit a buck is to position yourself upright in the saddle, or leaning slightly back, and to keep your hands a bit higher than usual while pushing the pony on with your legs. With experience you get wise to when a buck is coming and can often ride the pony forwards and out of it before he gets the chance to lower his head.

Do not let it become a habit, and certainly do not let your daughter encourage it because she thinks it is funny. A sharp reprimand and strong forward riding is the best solution; hitting the pony often makes him buck more.

Pulling

While it is very rare for a pony to bolt, most can get stronger than usual when they are excited. For instance, the pony who sees his friends cantering off ahead of him along the bridlepath is going to be eager to catch up with them.

Many riders profess to enjoy 'a good gallop', but there are very few places where it is safe to go at anything more than a fast canter. Bridlepaths, for instance, may also be used by walkers and by riders coming the other way, and, besides which, a rider should always feel that she can slow down without fighting the pony.

A pony who 'takes hold' in company should not be put in the situation where a race is inevitable. If he finds hacking out with other ponies exciting, get him used to it gradually and stick to walk and the occasional trot until he calms down. Keep early canters slow and short, preferably with a steady companion; some ponies only pull when they are behind another, so if this applies to your pony start off with him in front of the other pony and gradually get him used to cantering alongside. If he starts trying to race, bring both of them back to trot and then strike off into canter again when everything is under control.

The automatic reaction when riding a pulling pony is to pull back; this is the worst thing you can do, because he will inevitably be stronger. The rider should keep her weight slightly back and give intermittent checks on the reins, if necessary pushing one hand into the pony's neck as a brace and checking with the other. Bridging the reins is another useful technique, often used by jockeys and event riders. By making a 'bridge' across the pony's neck you ensure that he is pulling against himself rather than against the rider. If he really takes hold and there is enough room, the rider can try turning him in decreasing circles, being careful not to turn him so sharply that he loses his balance and falls over.

Some people will tell you to use a stronger bit, but do not do this without asking your instructor first. Used properly, a bit like a pelham can give the rider greater control and be more comfortable for a strong pony in situations like cross-country riding, but do not try one without supervision.

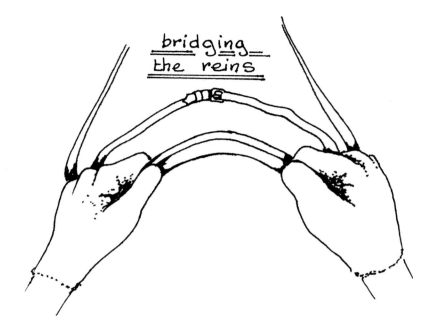

16 The Outgrown Pony

The time will eventually come when your daughter outgrows your first pony and needs a bigger one. In one way it is an exciting prospect, because hopefully she and the rest of the family will have learned a lot and be ready to take on new challenges. But inevitably it will also be a sad time, because unless you have a younger child who can start riding and looking after the first pony you will have to find him a new home. No matter how fond you have become of him, do not be tempted to keep him as a pet. A fit pony who has been happy working will only be bored when turned out in a field, and the best thing you can do for him is find another child who will have as much fun with him as your child has had.

An even worse alternative, in the case of a mare, is to have a foal from her simply because it seems like a nice idea. There is an old saying, 'Fools breed horses for wise men to ride', and though it is cynical, there is a lot of truth in it. One of the reasons ponies end up going for meat is that there is too much indiscriminate breeding.

From the financial point of view, the stud fee to the stallion's owner is only the beginning. You will also have the cost of vets' fees, extra food, separate grazing and perhaps stabling for the foal when it is weaned and the normal 'running costs' until it is old enough to break in. Unbroken youngsters need vaccinations and attention from the blacksmith just as often as older animals in work. A friend who breeds competition horses has just worked out that her four-day-old foal has already cost her £2,500. A pony mare who lives out will not run up bills like that for you, but it could still cost you more than buying someone else's unbroken three-year-old, so unless you have a particularly nice mare of known origin, and can afford to keep her foal until it is at least three years old, forget the idea of breeding with her.

Generally, the only two viable solutions are selling or loaning the pony to a

Unless you have a younger child who can start riding

suitable family. Loaning can be a good idea if you want the pony back in a year or two when younger brothers and sisters are old enough to look after him, but it should not really be looked on as a 'soft option' because you feel you cannot bear to part with him. It is tempting to think that no one will look after him as well, or love him as much, as you do, but think back to how quickly he settled with your family and you will have to admit there is no reason why he should not do the same with another one.

Sadly, you may not always be able to wave your pony goodbye to a nice new home. Ponies, like people, grow old, and when he is too old to work properly it is unfair to sell him. If you have any doubts about your pony's health or capabilities, ask your vet and take his advice, even if you do not like it. Many ponies live to a ripe old age, but if you know that yours is moving stiffly and cannot always get up easily, remember that retirement can simply mean prolonging the agony.

It is always heartbreaking when the vet advises that a pony should be put down, but this advice is never given lightly and a responsible owner will accept it. You should ask for the pony to be put down at his home; most yard owners will be sympathetic and will find a suitable time and place. They will probably even arrange for someone experienced to be on hand if you find the prospect too upsetting.

Remember that your pony will not know what is going to happen. As far as he is concerned, he is simply taken out of his stable and offered a bucket of his favourite food. As he lowers his head, the vet will shoot him with a humane killer, and death will be instant – the pony will be dead before he hits the floor. Your vet will also arrange for the disposal of the carcase, which of course is too big to be buried.

Loaning Your Pony

Any form of loaning should have the basis of a legal agreement drawn up by a solicitor and signed by both parties. Misunderstandings do arise, and life can become both complicated and unpleasant if it is a case of one person's word against another. Once you have satisfied yourself that the child who will be riding him and the place where he will be kept are suitable, rough out an agreement along the lines of the sample one given below (which is *only* for guidance).

> Loan agreement entered into on (date) between (name and address), hereafter known as the owner and (name and address) hereafter known as the borrower.
>
> This agreement relates to the 12.2 hh chestnut pony known as Ginger, registered name (if any). This pony is at all times to remain the property of (owner's name and address).
>
> The agreed loan period is for (duration) beginning on (date) and

can be terminated by either party on one/two/three months' written notice (as appropriate). The owner reserves the right to remove Ginger without notice if not satisfied that he is being kept according to the conditions of this agreement.

Ginger is to be kept at (address of stables) and the owner's permission must be given before he is moved.

The owner is to be responsible for insurance and for veterinary costs arising out of accident or illness, excluding vaccination costs.

The borrower is to be responsible for all feeding, stabling, grazing, farrier's and vaccination costs. The borrower agrees that Ginger should be attended by the farrier every six weeks and that organisation of this and all other day to day care are his responsibility.

Ginger may be used for activities specified in the owner's insurance policy (details) but must not be used for any outside this.

The owner reserves the right to visit Ginger once a month and to give 48 hours notice of his intention to visit.

Signed . . . . (owner) . . . . (borrower)
Address . . . .   Address . . . .
Date . . . .   Date . . . .

Let me emphasise yet again that this is only a guide and you should give careful thought to any additional stipulations that apply in your case before getting a proper agreement drawn up by a solicitor. For instance, is it vital that the pony is kept on shavings as opposed to straw, and must he be stabled at nights between certain dates? How often do you really want to visit him? It is important to strike a balance between keeping an eye on the pony's welfare, especially at first, and being such a nuisance to the family who have him on loan that it causes ill-feeling; no one wants to feel that they are being watched every minute of the day!

Another point to keep in mind is what you would do if the family suddenly said they could not keep your pony any longer and you would have to take him back. A loan agreement is good sense, but it does not help if the worst happens. Supposing one of the loan parents dies and the other cannot cope with your pony? Such a horrific situation is unlikely to arise – but it could.

Selling Your Pony

All in all, the best solution is usually to sell the pony. You can keep your options open by putting him on loan for, say, three months with the agreement that the loan family will buy him if they and you are satisfied all is well. Do be careful, though, that you do not enter into this sort of arrangement with someone who simply wants an extra pony for the summer holidays and who intends all along to send him back to you at the end of them. It has been known to happen!

You will want to do your best for the pony, and the simple way of doing this is to be as honest when you are selling him as you were when you bought him. Tell everyone you know that you are looking for a new home for him and make sure the news gets on to the Pony Club grapevine. With a bit of luck, you will find him a new family without too much trouble, especially if he has the reputation of being a kind, honest pony.

Do not be frightened to 'vet' any prospective new owners; it is quite reasonable to ask to see where the pony would be kept and to make sure his new rider will have someone more experienced to help her. When she tries him, make

There will be tears

allowances for the fact that she is less experienced than your daughter and is probably nervous about riding your pony in front of you – but if you are sure she is too novice to manage a pony on her own, say so in as tactful a way as possible! She might well learn as she goes along, but the pony is the one who will suffer as she makes mistakes.

When you have agreed a deal and the pony has passed the vet's inspection, it is a nice idea to write down a list of all the pony's characteristics that the new owners will find useful. For instance, is he used to his feet being picked out in a certain order or does he dislike his head being brushed? Little things like this make it easier for his new owners to handle him, as they may have done for you when you first bought him, and mean at least some things will stay the same for him even when he is in a new home. Finally, ask his new owners to let you know in a few days how he is getting on – you will probably want to visit him later and they will no doubt be pleased to welcome you, but give the new partnership a few weeks to settle down first.

Inevitably there will be tears when the pony goes, but you can console yourself that you have done the best you could for him. You can also look forward to the exciting prospect of buying your second pony, because once you have had a pony, life can never be the same without one!